In memory of Hyman and Dorothy Stone, life-long supporters of music at the *City Hall*, Sheffield, the *Free Trade Hall*, Manchester, the *Wigmore Hall*, the *Royal Festival Hall* and, of course, the *Royal Albert Hall*.

Text by Roger Williams
Picture Research by Suzanne Hodgart
Edited by Jonathan Stone
Foreword by HRH The Duke of Gloucester KG GCVO RIBA
Published by The Fitzhardinge Press for the Royal Albert Hall

THE ROYAL ALBERT HALL
A VICTORIAN MASTERPIECE
FOR THE 21ST CENTURY

First published in 2003 by
Fitzhardinge Press, a division of
Mantastar Limited, for the Royal
Albert Hall.

*British Library Cataloguing-in-
Publication Data*
A catalogue record for this book is
available from the British Library.

ISBN 1-8740-44554

Book designed by Untitled
www.untitledstudio.com

Book jacket, endpapers and dividers
by Alan Kitching RDI

Production by Robert Marcuson
Publishing Services.

Printed and bound in the United Kingdom.

Contents

The Royal Albert Hall rises in 'Albertopolis', the zenith of Victorian aspirations in the arts and sciences. It opens with high ideals, inexpensive subscription concerts and free Sunday afternoon organ recitals. Verdi brings his Requiem, Wagner oversees his own festival; Adelina Patti and Clara Butt are the glittering stars. The Wine Society is founded, pioneering experiments in Morse and electricity are carried out and Henry Morton Stanley reports on his African adventures.

Wrestling and boxing matches are introduced, a marathon is run round the arena and political meetings are interrupted by suffragettes. The Edwardian era is highlighted by extravagant charity balls and the Chelsea Arts Club stages the best-known annual revel. In summer, Londoners flock to see Samuel Coleridge-Taylor's *Hiawatha*. The largest assembly of musicians comes together to remember the lives lost on the Titanic; among the conductors are Edward Elgar, who in late life performs with the gifted young violinist, Yehudi Menuhin.

War time brings the Henry Wood Promenade Concerts to the Hall, and makes a name for their conductor, Sir Malcolm Sargent. Pop Proms follow in the Sixties when The Beatles and Rolling Stones share the same bill. Bob Dylan and Jimmy Hendrix play here, too, and Cream give their farewell concert. The Eurovision Song Contest is broadcast on colour television to Europe for the first time and Miss World takes a pasting. Reginald, Ronnie and Charlie Kray enter the boxing ring, but *The Sound of Music's* Trapp family brought a sweeter note.

Frank Zappa causes pop groups to be temporarily banned from the Hall, and the ageing crooner, Frank Sinatra, steps in to fill 'Francis Albert Hall'. Shirley Bassey and Eric Clapton also feel at home here. Sumo wrestling tournaments are held and the arena turns into an ice rink. Opera and ballet are seen for the first time at the Hall, with sell-out performances, and Cirque du Soleil becomes a regular date as the benefits of the £70 million redevelopment programme start to be felt.

Foreword
HRH The Duke of Gloucester *KG GCVO RIBA*

Anyone passing the Royal Albert Hall as they travel down Kensington Gore has to be aware of an almost circular building where square ones are the norm. It stands large and self confident with its terracotta finish and with a unique style that reflects the eclectic ambitions of the first half of the nineteenth century.

Who would expect to find such a vast concert hall so far from the centre of town? The story of its creation leads us to understand why it had to be the "Royal Albert Hall", and why its location was inevitable. The foresight of its creators, building this eccentric great structure in a country with a very thin musical tradition, but at the same time a growing middle class prepared to travel on the expanding railway network, both above and below ground, has proved itself over the decades.

Much larger than any theatre or opera house, the Hall has been the venue for many significant events; some parochial, often of national and frequently of international importance. This book demonstrates the transition of a building searching for a purpose, through the charisma of individuals who created traditions and, with the help of television, turned the Hall into a venue that plays a vital role in a nation with a thriving musical life of all kinds, to be found not only in this ancient monument but also in many newer halls, all around the country.

The Royal Albert Hall is much loved not just by the audiences that fill it – more than five thousand at a time – but also by those who perform in it. It is a similar story for the tennis players, boxers, ice skaters, even circus acts who know how to use the building to the best effect. The refurbishments for the 21st century leave the Royal Albert Hall able to maintain, and, even, enhance its traditions with confidence for the years ahead, while this book looks back on its eventful history and helps us to understand the building and all it has achieved.

Kensington Palace, London

Above The Duke of Gloucester, a trained architect, outside the building that was inspired by Prince Albert, his great-great-grandfather.

Opposite Looking north across the Hall's glass dome to the Albert Memorial, close to the site of the 1851 Great Exhibition.

Editor's Preface
A View to Tomorrow

The compelling and often evocative story told by Roger Williams, and the fascinating pictorial history of so many great moments in the 132-year history of the Hall, created by Suzanne Hodgart, merely prime the canvas for the future picture that tomorrow's history will paint.

Countless major international artistes and members of the Hall's staff have contributed to its success; regrettably, this book has been able to mention no more than a fraction of them.

Less than fifteen years ago, the Hall was, in many senses, moribund. Its fabric was in serious decline, and the very tired interior decoration was dowdy, unlovable and unloved. The auguries for the future of this Grade I building were inauspicious, as its competitors – especially on the classical musical front – capitalised on the woes of the doyen of British auditoria – the Royal Albert Hall. The Hall had, and still has, no annual central or local government grant, whether direct or indirect, as on a substantial scale do both its main London rivals, the Royal Festival Hall (including the Queen Elizabeth Hall), and the Barbican Hall. And, the threat to the Hall was compounded particularly on the non-classical-music front by the emergence of competing venues for pop and rock events.

The major National Lottery contribution to the extraordinarily creative south-side development and the restoration programme carried out over the past eight years has been greatly supported by the unique band of men and women, and corporates, the seat- and the box-holders, by some munificent grant-making trusts and by some eight thousand generous contributors, particularly from amongst the Hall's "regulars". It is an establishment that has – perhaps because of the catholic and the very unstuffy nature of the events and occasions that it has hosted – traditionally engendered affectionate feelings. But, the money alone would not have been enough without the vision and drive of the management and the Council. Halls have not only to have conductors who beat (time), but hearts that beat, too. Those responsible for the Hall realised that the unique combination of a marvellous building, the

anchor of the most significant classical music festival in the world, and truly state-of-the-art facilities could resurrect the Hall to its pre-eminent position. The underground excavations, brilliantly designed by BDP under the direction of their Martin Ward and managed by Taylor Woodrow Construction, and costing some £22 million, have been the foundation on which the benefits for audiences, performers, and event promoters have been built.

For audiences, there is less congestion; better auditorium ventilation and temperature control; and more bars and restaurants, rest rooms and entertaining rooms, with better facilities for the disabled. For the performers, dressing rooms, instrument storage and parking for stars have all been dramatically improved.

Event promoters have been made more welcome with improved accommodation, first-class service, a more cost-effective loading and unloading dock, as well as by the addition of 180 top-priced stalls, measurably improving the financial yield from hirings.

The Hall believes that the programme of major improvements completed in 2003 will allow it to say farewell to the hand-to-mouth existence of the past and to look positively forward to a future, not only of decent solvency, but to the fulfilment of Prince Albert's vision for the "Central Hall". The National Lottery has also shown vision to match that of Prince Albert and the Hall's contemporary Council and management, by enabling the facilities and improvements mentioned above to be put in place. As a result, rather than being just a "Receiving House" for the promotions of others, the Hall can take a proactive approach to educational work with children, to the commissioning of new choral and organ works, to which the Hall is so well suited, and to extending its involvement in the promotion (both on its own and on a co-operative basis) not only of the particularly successful ballet and opera, but on a wider canvas.

The management is also conscious that it must establish a sinking fund for the maintenance of the wonderful fabric so that never again will it ever face a major crisis, as when it started, quite literally, to crumble in 1987.

The Royal Albert Hall will, in early 2004, step proudly forward, and, rightly preening itself, will be able to say, "We are the finest arena for the 21st century, whether for music – both classical and pop, and those embracing both such as the brilliant Vienna Philharmonic/Bobby McFerrin concert at this year's Proms – for acrobats, for opera, for ballet, or for dinners, or for…. We are Britain's Hall for tomorrow".

Jonathan Stone, London, November, 2003

1867-
1900

Dreams of a cultural institution

*The Royal Albert Hall owes its first breath of
life to Prince Albert of Saxe-Coburg-Gotha who
embodied every virtuous Victorian aspiration.
Queen Victoria's Consort had been dead for six years
when she laid the foundation stone, by which
time plans were under way for a fitting memorial
to him in Kensington Gardens facing the Hall.
In Sir George Gilbert Scott's design a golden Albert
holds the programme of the 1851 Great Exhibition
that helped to fund the building of the Hall.
He is surrounded by figures representing Christian
and moral virtues, the geniuses of European
civilisation, four continents and eight bronzes of the
Arts and Sciences, to which the Hall was dedicated*

At the beginning of 1987 pieces of terracotta, loosened by frost, fell from the underside of the smoking gallery that runs round the upper levels of the Royal Albert Hall. It was a stark reminder that major expenditure on the maintenance of the building was long overdue. The Hall is of course a national institution, but it had always been financially self-sufficient. From early in its history, it has had to rely on an annual contribution from the 345 owners of the 1,266 privately-held seats to maintain the fabric of the building. Handed down on 999-year leases, the sales of these seats for £100 each had provided much of the money with which to build the Hall in the first place. After this visible sign of decay, the governing Council of the Hall faced the need to carry out a radical refurbishment of the building if its future was to be secured. With generous National Lottery grants and the financial support of seat holders and other benefactors, an eight-year, £70 million programme of building work to remodel parts and to refurbish the whole of the Hall would be completed in early 2004.

Privately-held seats are just one special feature of the largest purpose-built concert venue in the country, and they provide a link back to its foundation. This Grade I listed Victorian masterpiece had its origins in the Great Exhibition of 1851 held over the road in Hyde Park. Both were the products of the enthusiasm of Prince Francis Charles Augustus Albert Emmanuel of Saxe-Coburg-Gotha, Consort of Queen Victoria, and of Sir Henry Cole, a tireless – and sometimes tiresome – supporter and practitioner of the arts.

Prince Albert, born in 1819, had married his cousin Queen Victoria when they were both twenty-one. A model family man, he became the father of nine and the perfect Victorian, instilled with duty and the pursuit of self-improvement, in himself as well as in others. Henry Cole, born in Bath in 1808, had been employed in various government departments since the age of fourteen, and he possessed a consummate ability to make things happen. He had designed china for the Minton pottery in Stoke, founded the *Journal of Design and Manufactures*, published books and is credited with producing the first Christmas card. Short and round with whiskers that made him look like Uncle Sam, he and his West-London project became so well known that the French novelist Prosper Merimée once joked that a letter addressed to "Mr South Kensington, England" would reach him.

Cole shared the Prince Consort's view that the rapidly changing industrial world should be harnessed to the arts, and he asked him to become President of the Royal Society for the Encouragement of Arts, Manufactures and Commerce (now the Royal Society of Arts). With Albert at its head, the Society became a driving force behind the 1851 Great Exhibition of the Works and Industry of All Nations. It would be, the Prince

Consort believed, "a true test and a living picture of the point of development at which the whole of mankind has arrived, and a starting point from which all nations will be able to direct their further exertions."

Nobody would be excluded from Albert's vision of human progress and he proposed that entry to the Exhibition's Crystal Palace should be inexpensive, if not free. Such a radical view was not shared by *The Times*, which thought this would attract such unsavoury characters that "the Season would be ruined", while the Duke of Wellington, the official Ranger of Hyde Park, proposed deploying 15,000 troops and a substantial police force to keep the common herd under control. It was, after all, just three years since the Chartist outbursts in the Year of Revolutions when Wellington had put metal shutters on his Hyde Park Corner home, confirming his nickname of the Iron Duke.

Prince Albert's faith in his wife's subjects was not misplaced. A single case of theft was the only reported incident among the six million visitors in the 140 days of the Exhibition. Such a resounding success proved that the public had an appetite and curiosity for the culture and achievements of the world around them. To Cole and Prince Albert, this was clear evidence that there was much more to be done. As a starting point, £150,000 from the profits, together with a government grant of £177,500, were used by the Commissioners of the Great Exhibition to buy a 50-acre Gore estate opposite the exhibition site in Kensington Gore where a complex of public buildings devoted to the arts and sciences could be built. Among them would be a great Central Hall for the Arts and Sciences.

The Birth of Albertopolis
Prince Albert lost no time on plans for what would become South Kensington's "Albertopolis", ultimately incorporating the Imperial College of Science, Technology and Medicine, the Royal College of Art, Victoria and Albert Museum, Science Museum, Natural History Museum, Royal College of Music and Royal Geographical Society. As a first step, the Commissioners rented the northern half of the Gore estate to the Royal Horticultural Society. Here the Prince supervised the installation of the largest formal garden in the country around which he imagined his institutions would grow. Captain Francis Fowke designed and built a new conservatory, a 270-foot-long Crystal Palace in miniature on the north side of the estate. It was subsequently to serve as a large and luminous lobby for the Hall. Military men had been building the empire, and the Royal Engineers with whom Fowke had served produced men of creativity as well as ability. More than that, Fowke, born in Belfast in 1823, designed the National Gallery in Dublin and the Museum of Science and Art in Edinburgh. With Cole, he also

produced the early plans of the South Kensington Museum, which was to become the Victoria and Albert Museum with a wing named after Cole in recognition of his contribution.

A few months after Fowke's conservatory was opened, Prince Albert died of typhoid, aged forty-two. Distraught, the Queen was convinced he had caught the fever in the gardens where he had spent so much of the last two years of his life. His death did not materially alter the projects; but it was a diversion, not least because energy and funds were channelled towards a suitable memorial to Albert to stand in the park opposite the Gore estate. This glorious task was given to the great Gothic architect George Gilbert Scott, designer of St Pancras railway station, whose plans for the Hall had been rejected.

Four years later, in 1865, plans for the Hall drawn up by Cole and Fowke were approved by the Queen. Lack of funds and a sense of reality had chipped away at their initial hope that it might seat 30,000. This figure had become a more realistic 7,000 and today the Hall comfortably seats just over 5,250 with three tiers of boxes, or loggias, between the stalls and balcony seats, and a gallery for standing or promenading its rim. The Hall would be managed by a governing body acting under a Royal Charter, granted on April 8, 1867, and it would be built on land rented from the Commissioners of the Great Exhibition on a 999-year lease for a shilling (5p) a year, a sum that has never increased.

In the matter of large building works, London had some catching up to do. This was the Golden Age of English provincial culture, and the rapidly-expanding cities of the north were putting up unprecedented municipal buildings. Birmingham's Town Hall, completed in the 1830s, could hold concerts for 3,000 – 9,000 if the seats were removed. In 1855 Liverpool's immense St George's Hall resounded to what was claimed to be the first modern concert organ in the world, ordered from Henry Willis's stand at the Great Exhibition and played by Dr William Thomas Best. A year later Manchester's Free Trade Hall was opened.

Many of these buildings were neo-Classical fantasies, pagan temples to decent Christian culture and civic pride, which had come into fashion after extended peace in Europe had made travelling popular. The inspiration for the South Kensington Hall came from the Roman arenas at Arles and Nîmes in Provence, which Cole visited with Fowke and the pottery manufacturer Colin Minton Campbell the year before finalising their plan.

Unfortunately, Fowke died shortly after the plan's approval, to be replaced by a colleague, Colonel Henry Darracott Scott, another Royal Engineer, who was on the committee carrying out Fowke's design for the South Kensington Museum. Scott modified Fowke's drawings for the Hall and it was his idea to install offices and ancillary buildings inside its circumference to give the façade an uninterrupted run. The North, West and East Porches had arches large enough for carriages picking up and putting down passengers. The rooms above them would eventually include studio space for the West Theatre, now the Elgar Room, which would become home to the Central School of Speech and Drama, and practice rooms for the National Training School of Music, the fledgling Royal College of Music. The South Porch would be attached to the RHS conservatory.

Building the Hall

Still overshadowed by a dark cloud of mourning, Queen Victoria laid the foundation stone on May 20, 1867, surprising the thousands assembled by attaching the words "Royal Albert" to the Hall for the Arts and Sciences, an addition that of course had to remain. She returned only once during the four years of building, trying out the twenty seats she had purchased in the grand tier for the Royal Box and listening to some songs. It was on this occasion that she gave her only recorded comment on the Hall. "It looks like the British constitution," she said.

There was no fear that Albert would be forgotten. Above an 800-foot-long terracotta frieze that encircled the building sixty-five feet from the ground, an inscription reads in part: "THIS HALL WAS ERECTED FOR THE ADVANCEMENT OF THE ARTS AND SCIENCE AND WORKS OF INDUSTRY OF ALL NATIONS IN FULFILMENT OF THE INTENTION OF ALBERT PRINCE CONSORT." The frieze took two years to make. Seven artists provided designs in fifty-foot lengths with allegorical and historical scenes and figures, including Michelangelo and James Watt. Photographs of these designs were dispatched to students at the South Kensington Museum to make the ceramic mosaics that would form the lively figurative pageant.

The Hall's most daring architectural feature was the roof, an unprecedented double-skinned dome of iron and glass. It was constructed at Fairbairn Engineering in Ardwick, Manchester, dismantled, transported south and placed over the Hall. After the building had been evacuated, Scott and a colleague knocked out the wedges of the supporting scaffolding and the 400-ton iron structure settled into place, moving a mere half an inch.

Measuring 219 feet by 185 feet, the Hall required 80,000 buff-coloured terracotta blocks and six million red bricks, the first of which had been laid by Mrs Henry Cole. The feats of engineering overseen by Scott included a massive ventilation and heating system and the installation of 11,000 gas burners that could all be lit in ten seconds. The focus of the auditorium was Henry Willis's 150-ton organ, a high altar of sound with nine miles of pipes and two steam engines to drive its bellows. It was the largest and most versatile instrument in the world.

A month before the Hall opened, several thousand Londoners attended a free test concert that revealed echoes, blind spots and other acoustic defects. As a result a calico velarium was stretched below the dome, suffusing the sound and restricting the direct flood of daylight from the half acre of glass. It would stay there, gathering dust, for nearly eighty years.

Not everything was ready by the time of the opening ceremony. Niches for busts of Victoria and Albert on the North Porch remained empty, and they are yet to be filled. But for a coat of paint and a few other finishing touches, the Hall was otherwise completed on time, coming in £252 under its £200,000 budget.

The Opening
The management of the Hall put Sir Michael Costa in charge of the opening concert and later appointed Charles François Gounod as first resident conductor of the choir. Nobody expected a British musician to take these positions. Since the death of Henry Purcell in 1695, England had become known abroad as "The Land without Music"; famous composers and conductors, such as the German, Charles Hallé, whose renowned orchestra was playing at Manchester's Free Trade Hall, invariably came from the Continent. Costa was a Neapolitan and had been conducting at Covent Garden Theatre since it had been renamed the Royal Italian Opera House in 1847. Gounod was a windfall from the Franco-Prussian War. The only significant evidence of home-grown talent was William Best, persuaded down from Liverpool to install the organ and play at the opening.

At midday on Wednesday, March 29, 1871, the dapper figure of Henry Cole came on stage to call for hush from the audience of 7,000. He raised an arm towards the brass lens of a camera set in the crimson and turquoise Royal Box and everyone held their breath. The picture taken, the audience relaxed into laughter and chatter. They were in a high state of anticipation. It wouldn't be long before the royal party arrived.

Unfortunately the photograph has not survived, and if it had, it would not reflect the dazzling colour of the occasion, nor the scent, for the Hall's sophisticated air venting system wafted *eau de cologne* everywhere. People had journeyed from central London either by carriage or via the new underground station at South Kensington, making their way up to the Hall through the Royal Horticultural Society Gardens. Among them was the man from the *Sunday Times*, whose description of the audience was particularly florid: "If you half shut your eyes and gazed at the tier upon tier of bright colours you might almost fancy the May show of the pelargoniums and rhododendrons and American plants of the Botanic. Pale rose, light mauve, lilac, lip red, shell pink, turquoise, celadon, maiden blush, pearl grey and creamy white. These were the prevailing colours that might be seen in the amphitheatre, where they seemed to rise parterre upon parterre." Additional colour was added by a delegation from Burma, the

first ever to visit "the land of the pale faces", according to the *Morning Post*. "Attired in closely fitting robes, of a delicate amber hue, turbans of spotless white and wearing lemon-coloured gloves, the Burmese gentlemen were the most honoured of the guests, if it is an honour to be stared at through double lorgnettes for an hour at a time."

But there were dull dressers, too, much to the distress of the *Sunday Times* reporter. "The only thing that marred this pretty, Dresden china-like delicacy of the ladies' dresses was the black coats of that portion of the audience who came not in uniform. Certainly there should be an order on such occasions that all the gentlemen who could not go in uniform should be obliged to don brown holland pinafores or French blouses for the occasion."

Among the men in black were the Prime Minister, William Gladstone, the Tory leader, Benjamin Disraeli, the mayors of towns that had contributed to the Great Exhibition and some of those who paid just one guinea to peer down from the gallery. The 500 members of the orchestra and 1,200 singers also lacked colour, causing the *Sunday Times* continuing distress: "The ladies in the chorus do not present so gay an appearance as those of the audience, and one or two blots of positive colour, in the way of scarlet opera cloaks – looking almost like 'kisses' of red sealing wax – by no means improved the general effect. The orchestra was one hopeless mass of black."

The Queen herself, who arrived thirty-five minutes after the photograph had been taken, was also dressed in black, as she had been since the death of Albert. Her only concession to the gaiety of the occasion was a few white flowers in her black bonnet.

According to the Press Association telegram that was sent around the world, she arrived looking fatigued and unwell, in contrast to Princess Louise, eighth of her nine children, who was radiant from her recent marriage to the fully-kilted Marquess of Lorne. Others disgorged from the eleven royal coaches included ladies of the bedchamber, maids of honour, the Master of the Horse and the Gold and Silver Sticks in Waiting. Settling on to a platform in the auditorium around the Queen's throne, they were greeted with the thunder of Dr Best at the organ and the massed choir singing the National Anthem. The Queen seemed to cheer a little, but she failed to find the strength to do her duty and it was left to the twenty-nine-year-old Prince of Wales, raising his voice unnecessarily, to declare the Hall open. His father was undoubtedly present in spirit and was almost incarnate when Costa picked up the baton to conduct *L'Invocazione all'Armonia*, one of Albert's own works, a thinnish piece, but "with felicitous thoughts very suggestive of the purity, sweetness and refinement of the composer's mind", according to one newspaper report.

Costa himself had composed a piece especially for the occasion, with lyrics by John Oxenford adapted from the Psalms.

Everything went well. The cheers and hurrahs that greeted the performances that afternoon were explosive. All complaints about the Hall and the Queen's morbid attachment to her husband's memory fell away. Even the acoustics were pronounced perfect, not just by enraptured fans, but also by the journals such as *The Architect*, though the last "Amen" delivered by the Bishop of London was said to have been heard twice.

Perhaps the most gratified person in the Hall was the man who had spent two decades bringing all this about. That evening the Queen noted in her diary, "Good Mr Cole was quite crying with enthusiasm and delight."

What Happens Next?
Preparations for the opening of the Royal Albert Hall had been so momentous that what followed was in danger of seeming an anticlimax. The building was enormous, the possibilities endless, but that was no help. "The question which must arise in the mind of every visitor who gazes at it, is 'What will they do with it?'" *The Times* was not alone in its concern that the Hall might become another Victorian white elephant, an extravagant solution in search of a problem like Brunel's "Great Eastern", the world's largest vessel, recently reduced to laying cables across the Atlantic and soon to be mothballed in Milford Haven.

What was not disputed was that the Hall should give popular public music performances for as many people as possible to enjoy. At first there were daily performances on the organ, military bands from Europe, choral series, and concerts in aid of the National Training School of Music, which in 1875 became the first occupants of the elaborately decorated building on the west side of the Hall. (Now privately owned, this building was occupied by the Royal College of Organists from 1904 to 1990.)

What the Hall was undoubtedly good for was a lot of noise. Military bands made a tremendous noise, and so did massed choirs, encouraged by a thunderous organ. If England had not produced any music of note for more than a century, it was to produce an outstanding choir master in Sir Joseph Barnby, who took over from Gounod as conductor at the Hall the year after it opened. Born in York and sustained by a vigorous constitution, Barnby had become only the second music master to be appointed at Eton College, setting to music *Carmen Etonense*, the school song. But Barnby was no musical snob and as master of more than a thousand voices of the amateur Royal Albert Hall Choral Society, later simply the Royal Choral Society, he was responsible for some memorable occasions.

His Yorkshire background made him well aware of the appetite for choral singing that had been sweeping the densely populated industrial cities of the north. By now no town in Yorkshire, Lancashire or Derbyshire was without a choral society,

no church nor town hall without an oratorio. What helped to make choral singing popular was the invention in the 1840s of the "tonic sol-fa" to help ordinary people to read music. Taking the key note as a movable doh, a tune could be notated simply in terms of doh, ray, me, fah, sol, lah, te, or just the initials, with a higher or lower octave indicated by a small tick (d_1 or d^1), so that the National Anthem's opening notes, for example, could be rendered as d d d r t_1 d r. There were those, of course, who found such simplicity far too prosaic, but Barnby was in sympathy with the system, which he declared he had used since childhood.

Another important factor in spreading choral music was the availability of hymn books and song sheets. In 1830 a copy of Handel's Messiah cost a guinea (£1.05p). By 1880 you could pick up a copy for a shilling (5p). *Hymns Ancient and Modern*, which to date has sold more than 170 million copies, was first published the year that the Hall's foundation stone was laid, and many of the first hymn books had tonic sol-fah annotations. The religious revival that was sweeping Wales coincided with the arrival of the tonic sol-fa, creating "The Land of the Great Choirs" and a fashion for christening boys Handel. Two Eisteddfodau were held at the Hall, in 1887 and 1909.

After two decades at his post, Barnby was asked why music had become so popular in Britain. "I account for it largely because the puritan prejudices have been overcome," he said, "and that we are beginning to regard music as a great social and intellectual force. We are still, of course, far behind most of the other Continental nations but the next generation compared with whom we shall only rank as pygmies, will doubtless be able to hold their own against any rivals."

With the arguable exception of Handel and his Messiah, a Good Friday concert established by Barnby that continues to this day, blockbusters involving the Royal Choral Society were all by Continentals: Mendelssohn's Elijah, Wagner's Parsifal, Requiems by Mozart and Dvořák and Bach's St Matthew Passion, sung during Holy Week and involving the whole audience. Barnby was said to have "discovered" Dvořák and when the Bohemian composer arrived to conduct his Stabat Mater, "thundering and lasting applause" left him speechless. Anton Bruckner came to play the organ, and so did Camille Saint-Saëns, organist at the Madeleine in Paris and a former pupil of Gounod, whose series of recitals was warmly received.

Celebrated Conductors
Another major piece to arrive from the Continent was *Requiem to Manzoni*, which was brought to the Hall by its creator, Giuseppe Verdi, on its debut tour in 1875. The sixty-one-year-old Italian was not enamoured of the idea of London, which he thought a "sad, dreary place at all times". It was feared that he would not

attract enough people to fill the Hall, and it was suggested that it might play better at Covent Garden where that other great hero of Italian independence, Garibaldi, had been lionised on a visit ten years earlier. Verdi would not hear of any other venue, however, and there must have been many Italian immigrants from Clerkenwell who took the Metropolitan underground from Farringdon to South Kensington for the Requiem's two performances in May, which were extended by a further two by public demand. "Rarely have we seen an audience more thoroughly pleased," said *The Times*.

Two years later the Wagner Festival brought the German composer to London. Bayreuth had just become home to his epic operas and he had hoped never again to have his works performed in a concert room, but a lack of funds drove him back. "Yet he could not help being pleased," said *The Times* on his arrival, "at the opportunity afforded him of conducting a selection from his works before an auditory from whom he was sure of an intelligent sympathy." Wagner took an instant liking to the South Kensington venue, and he later told an English acquaintance, "On entering the Hall for the first time, it struck me at once as the beau ideal of a place for performing Beethoven's Ninth Symphony in a manner and on a scale really worthy of the great master. If I had to conduct it, the choir would occupy the gallery and the orchestra I would arrange in the centre of the arena. The effect would be stupendous."

Wagner was not given the chance to attempt this arrangement of a concert-in-the-round, but the festival of selections from his operas, for which he shared the conductor's podium with Hans Richter, was a resounding success. "Indiscriminate applause was bestowed on piece after piece," said *The Times*, describing the lack of scenic accessories of the operas as a gain, not a loss. "Presented as at the Albert Hall, the supreme beauty of the music told its own story, and was appreciated on its own account."

Star Singers
Opera, or anything remotely theatrical, was not then considered appropriate for the Hall. The closest it came to theatre was in such events as The Shakespeare Show in 1884, when there were *tableaux vivants* of scenes from *The Winter's Tale*. Nor was the Hall ever allowed to become anything resembling a music hall. Its most popular singers were opera stars who had to leave their acting talents at the door. None was better known or liked than Adelina Patti, the most celebrated soprano of the second half of the 19th century. Born in Madrid in 1843, she moved with her Italian parents to New York as a child. Her European debut was at Covent Garden at the age of 18, and she eventually set up home in the magnificent Craig-y-Nos Castle in Wales. She commanded thousands of pounds for each appearance, sometimes insisting on being paid in gold. People came to see

her jewellery sparkle as much as they came to hear her sing, and security guards would sometimes accompany her on stage.

Her first appearance at the Royal Albert Hall was in 1882 and it became a regular booking over the next two decades. She had no concerns about singing popular songs. "Some people have pooh-poohed the idea of the difficulty of a simple melody," she said. "But it is more difficult to sing because of its demands upon the development of the voice." *Home Sweet Home* from the 1823 opera *Clari – the Maid of Milan* by the American John Howard Payne with music by the London composer Henry Rowley Bishop, regularly brought the house down. Among the many thousands who went to South Kensington to see the celebrated soprano was George Bernard Shaw, perhaps before or after a visit to the actress Mrs Patrick Campbell in nearby 33 Kensington Square. In a concert review, he wrote, "On Saturday afternoon the Albert Hall was filled by the attraction of our still adored Patti. The concert was a huge success: there were bouquets, rapture, effusions, kissing of children, graceful sharing of the applause with obbligato players – in short, the usual exhibition of the British bourgeoisie in the part of Bottom, and the *prima donna* in the part of Titania." Her "last appearance" at the Hall was in 1906, but she returned a final time in 1914, aged seventy-one.

Ten years after Patti first appeared, her successor made her debut at the Hall. Dame Clara Butt had been a student at the Royal College of Music and was supposedly another "discovery" of Barnby. Her extraordinary contralto voice, perhaps rather deep and ponderous for today's taste, won nothing but admiration, not least from Sir Thomas Beecham who claimed it to was so powerful that on a clear day it could be heard on the other side of the English Channel. Like Patti, Butt was committed to song: "The true English style is that of the minstrel school, which I take to mean the ability to render a simple song or ballad with directness and sincerity, an ability distinct and very different from that of the average opera singer, to whom the art that conceals is not of much use. The English style is more lyrical than dramatic."

Her theme tune was the hymn *Abide With Me*, written by Henry Lyte, pastor of Lower Brixham in Devon but not known about until put to music and published by William Henry Monk in his *Hymns Ancient and Modern*. Unlike Patti, Butt was born in the gramophone age, and in a few decades she would soon be selling records of *Abide with Me* and other songs by the thousand.

Clara Butt raised the roof for the First National Brass Band Championships, held in 1900 with Sir Arthur Sullivan conducting. By now there were around 250 brass bands in England, and it was time that they found a legitimate music platform in the capital. The Hall was packed to bursting and an estimated 5,000 remained outside, desperate for a ticket. Eleven champion bands played and John Henry Iles, the organiser, recalled, "The opening was with Clara Butt singing the verses, and the great audience, massed bands, organ and drums of the Guards Brigade joining in one immense and thrilling chorus of *Onward Christian Soldiers*. Sir Arthur was conducting, and told me with tears in his eyes that he had difficulty in carrying on. That tremendous crescendo roll of sixty drummers of the Guards Brigade leading up to the massed chorus was something few in the vast audience would easily have forgotten."

Royal Visitors and Entertainments
As President of the Commissioners of the Hall, the Prince of Wales enjoyed many hours in the Royal Box, attending balls and masonic meetings as well as listening to music. It was also left to him to entertain visiting relations, who included most of the crowned heads of Europe, and they were always keen to visit the world's largest concert hall. In June 1873 the Shah and Czarina of Persia were the object of great curiosity. Entering through the conservatory of the Royal Horticultural Society "crowded with fair women and brave men", they were treated to Persian melodies played on the organ by Dr Best. The high point of the evening, however, was when five shafts of lime light were beamed down from the gallery "illuminating the scene with dazzling brilliancy". This had been organised by Messrs Tisley and Spiller using batteries placed on the roof. The Shah was aware of such innovations emanating from this versatile Hall because the previous year the Society of Telegraph Engineers had hired it to demonstrate a Morse link to Karachi via Persia. Permanent electric lighting arrived in 1888, the year that the Presidency of the Hall passed to the Prince of Wales's more musical younger brother Alfred, Duke of Edinburgh. In 1872 he had founded the Royal Amateur Orchestral Society and he occasionally played first violin in its concerts.

Balls, masonic meetings and other private occasions that needed to be exclusive led to negotiations with the seat-holders. Die-hards wanted to sit in on any event, while those with seats in the stalls objected to their being physically removed to extend the arena. Eventually it was agreed that they should give up the right to their seats on ten days each year in exchange for a share of the rental of the Hall. Since then their rights have been subject to a number of further restrictions. The private loggias, or boxes, meanwhile, had all been decorated to their owners' tastes, creating what should have been a series of delightful drawing rooms. The urge to outdo each other, however, resulted in such outrageous distractions that in the end uniformity had to be imposed.

The Hall was hired for exhibitions, meetings, *conversazioni*, prize-givings, lectures and dinners for institutes and societies. Art exhibitions were well suited to the well-lit gallery. In the cellars a large quantity of Portuguese wine was overlooked in a Food and Wine Exhibition in 1874; helping to distribute it in a series of subsequent dinners, Colonel Scott became the unwitting founder of The Wine Society. The American journalist Henry Morton Stanley, whose exploration into Africa to find Dr Livingstone had been funded by the Royal Geographical Society, told its members of his adventures, while the Norwegian explorer Fridtjof Nansen outlined to the Society his plan to cross the Greenland ice cap, east to west, which was loudly condemned.

There were demonstrations of cycling, and the military showed off its skills in assaults of arms that included wrestling, boxing, swordsmanship and sabre practices, gymnastics, lance exercises, tug-of-wars and life saving from a supposed fire. Charity balls and money-raising ventures included an event organised by The Young Helpers' League, when 17,402 children "from happy homes" from all over the world came together to aid those less fortunate than themselves. *Truth* magazine put on regular Christmas toy fairs to raise money for London's hospitals and workhouses, with around 35,000 visitors a day.

Attracting an Audience
By the end of Victoria's reign, the Royal Albert Hall was firmly on the cultural map of London, but efforts still had to be made to persuade people to undertake the journey to South Kensington. There were plenty of other amusements for Londoners. From 1895 these included an annual ten-week series of popular concerts at the newly-built Queen's Hall in Langham Place conducted by a twenty-six-year-old Londoner, Henry J. Wood.

From the early days the Hall had offered inducements. Combined rail and seat tickets were sold on the Metropolitan Line, now the Circle Line: shilling gallery tickets included free third-class transport, two-and-sixpenny balcony seats second class, and stalls first-class, in each case the railway taking sixpence for its troubles. Even so, the station was fifteen minutes' walk away and unpleasant in foul weather, especially during the infamous smogs. Conditions improved with a purpose-built tunnel at South Kensington station, which today leads to the Science Museum. It was originally designed to emerge at the Royal Horticultural Society Gardens, where Italianate arcades provided shelter as far as Fowke's conservatory that served as a foyer to the Hall.

In 1889, however, the Royal Horticultural Society encountered financial difficulties and its lease of the gardens came to an end. The conservatory and the arcades were sold off and dismantled. This meant the loss of a useful building that provided the additional services of refreshments, cloakrooms and simply space, all of which would be missed. But it had to give way to the building work that was day by day bringing Prince Albert's dreams nearer to fulfilment.

Above The Great Exhibition in Hyde Park in 1851 attracted six million visitors, encouraging Prince Albert to establish a centre to promote the understanding and appreciation of the arts and sciences.

Below The 50-acre Gore estate was bought with the help of profits from the Great Exhibition. Stretching from the park to Cromwell Road, this is where 'Albertopolis' would be built, starting with the Royal Horticultural Society Gardens (*right*) where Albert spent much his time.

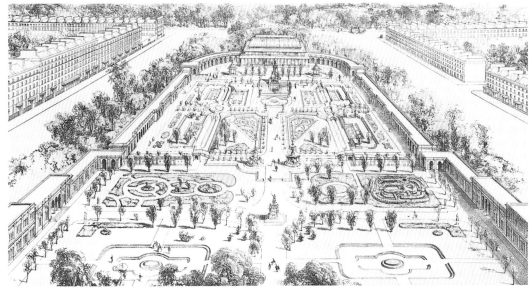

Life-size portraits of Queen Victoria and Prince Albert were painted between 1844 and 1855 by Frederick Newenham and shown at the Royal Academy. They now hang inside the Hall's main entrance.

Above In an early illustration, Albert's Central Hall for the Arts and Sciences had a solid roof. The final design, by Henry Cole and Captain Francis Fowke, was based on Roman amphitheatres.

Right Cole, on the left of the picture, is seen discussing with Fowke plans for an exhibition in the RHS Gardens in 1862. Fowke had designed the RHS conservatory and what was to become the Victoria and Albert Museum, but he died before construction of the Hall began.

"It is my wish that this hall should bear his name to whom it will have owed its existence, and be called 'The Royal Albert Hall of Arts and Sciences.'" – Queen Victoria on laying the foundation stone, May 20, 1867

Left Six years after Albert's death, Queen Victoria laid the foundation stone, unexpectedly adding the name 'Royal Albert' to the Hall of Arts and Sciences. Thousands turned out for the ceremony, held within a huge marquee, and cannons were fired in Hyde Park.

Below left An early idea of how the interior might look, before a glass dome was decided on.

This page A public building of unprecedented size takes shape under the direction of Colonel Henry Scott. Rising in the background is the Albert Memorial by George Gilbert Scott, whose designs for the Hall had been rejected.

The dome is assembled at Ardwick, Manchester. With a half acre of glass, it would bathe the Hall in light and give it a true feeling of a Roman amphitheatre. Acoustically, however, it was a disaster, and the sky soon had to be blotted out with a velarium.

Above The 400-ton iron frame is erected and tested on the ground near the Manchester works of the Fairbairn Engineering Company before being dismantled and carried to London by road and re-assembled (*opposite*). It was supported only at its rim.

Right Work progresses on the site of Gore House, which had functioned as a restaurant during the Great Exhibition. Beyond it are the Royal Horticultural Society Gardens and Fowke's conservatory, to which the Hall's South Porch was attached. The photograph appears to have been taken from the top of the Albert Memorial.

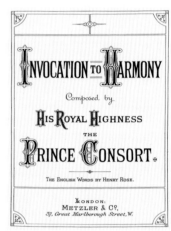

Above On March 29, 1871, Queen Victoria arrived for the opening concert, but it was left to the Prince of Wales (*pictured opposite*) to step forward and declare the Hall open.

Below The opening was a colourful occasion. All society was present and *eau de cologne* was pumped through the ventilation system to make the atmosphere even sweeter. Prince Albert appeared in spirit with a song he had composed (*above right*), conducted by Sir Michael Costa.

THE ILLUSTRATED LONDON NEWS

REGISTERED AT THE GENERAL POST-OFFICE FOR TRANSMISSION ABROAD.

No. 1644.—VOL. LVIII.　　　SATURDAY, APRIL 8, 1871.　　　PRICE FIVEPENCE

OPENING OF THE ROYAL ALBERT HALL BY THE QUEEN: THE PRINCE OF WALES DECLARING THE HALL OPEN.

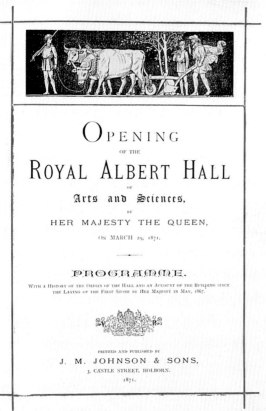

Above This is the earliest surviving photograph of the interior of the Hall. More than 1,250 seats were privately owned, bought at £100 each to help fund the building.

Left and below A programme of the opening concert and a paperweight were among the first souvenirs.

Science illuminated the arts in 1873
during a state visit of the Shah and
Czarina of Persia, guests of the
Prince of Wales. During the evening
concert, the platform was lit by five
shafts of lime light, each produced
by a battery of fifty cells on the roof.

INVENZIONE — WALTZ.

Played with Unprecedented Success, at the
INTERNATIONAL INVENTIONS EXHIBITION
by the Bands of the
GRENADIER GUARDS AND ROYAL IRISH CONSTABULARY,
also at the
CRYSTAL PALACE. ALBERT PALACE. HYDE PARK CONCERTS,
and by the Band of the
HONOURABLE ARTILLERY COMPANY.

BY
LEONARD GAUTIER.

DEDICATED BY SPECIAL PERMISSION
TO
EDWARD CUNLIFFE-OWEN ESQ.

ENT. STA HALL.

LONDON.
FREDERICK PITMAN, 20 & 21, PATERNOSTER ROW, E.C.
WEST END AGENTS - J B CRAMER & C° 201, REGENT STREET, W.

PIANO SOLO	2/NET
DUET	2/
VIOLIN & PIANO	1/6
FLUTE & PIANO	1/6
SEPTET	1/
FULL ORCHESTRA	1/6
MILITARY BAND	5/

Left For the purposes of many exhibitions, the Royal Horticultural Society Gardens and Royal Albert Hall were regarded as a single venue. 'Invenzione' were usually simply concerts of newly 'invented' music.

Right The plan for the 1886 Colonial and Indian Exhibition shows how the Hall was linked with the RHS conservatory and gardens. At the opening concert Madame Albani sang a piece specially written by Alfred Lord Tennyson and set to music by Arthur Sullivan.

Overleaf A stereo card of the RHS conservatory and Hall. Seen through stereoscopes, these dual photos became three-dimensional images. Stereoscopes had been a hit of the Great Exhibition. This photograph, like the one of the Hall's opening concert (now lost), was taken by the London Stereoscopic Company and sold for a shilling, 1s 6d coloured. They made a fortune for the company, which was one of the world's largest photographic houses. In 1884 its owner, George Swan Nottage, became Lord Mayor of London.

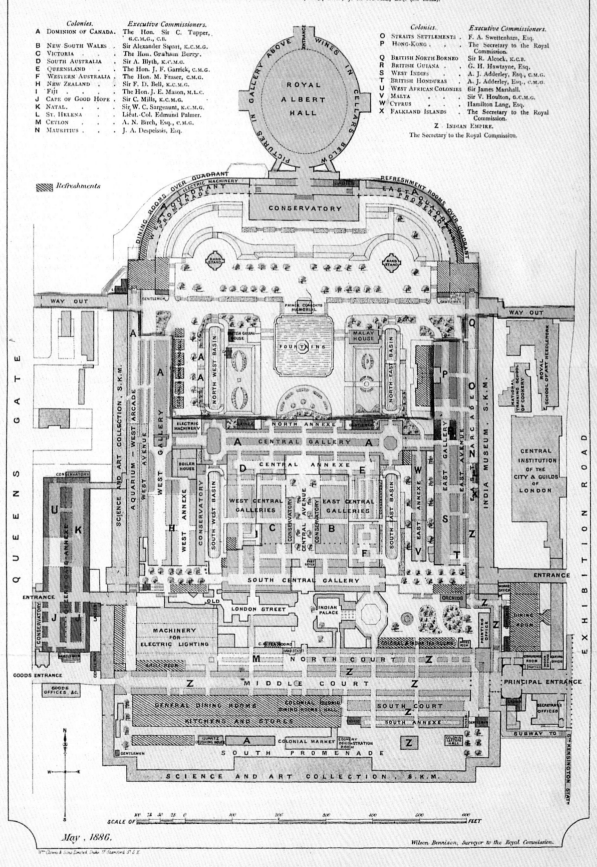

ROYAL COMMISSION FOR THE
COLONIAL AND INDIAN EXHIBITION, LONDON, 1886.

Executive President—HIS ROYAL HIGHNESS THE PRINCE OF WALES, K.G.

Secretary—SIR PHILIP CUNLIFFE-OWEN, K.C.M.G., C.B., C.I.E.

Assistant Secretaries—EDWARD CUNLIFFE-OWEN, Esq., B.A.; J. R. ROYLE, Esq. (for India).

	Colonies.	Executive Commissioners.
A	DOMINION OF CANADA.	The Hon. Sir C. Tupper, G.C.M.G., C.B.
B	NEW SOUTH WALES	Sir Alexander Stuart, K.C.M.G.
C	VICTORIA	The Hon. Graham Berry.
D	SOUTH AUSTRALIA	Sir A. Blyth, K.C.M.G.
E	QUEENSLAND	The Hon. J. F. Garrick, C.M.G.
F	WESTERN AUSTRALIA	The Hon. M. Fraser, C.M.G.
H	NEW ZEALAND	Sir F. D. Bell, K.C.M.G.
I	FIJI	The Hon. J. E. Mason, M.L.C.
J	CAPE OF GOOD HOPE	Sir C. Mills, K.C.M.G.
K	NATAL	Sir W. C. Sargeaunt, K.C.M.G.
L	ST. HELENA	Lieut.-Col. Edmund Palmer.
M	CEYLON	A. N. Birch, Esq., C.M.G.
N	MAURITIUS	J. A. Despeissis, Esq.

	Colonies.	Executive Commissioners.
O	STRAITS SETTLEMENTS	F. A. Swettenham, Esq.
P	HONG-KONG	The Secretary to the Royal Commission.
Q	BRITISH NORTH BORNEO	Sir R. Alcock, K.C.B.
R	BRITISH GUIANA	G. H. Hawtayne, Esq.
S	WEST INDIES	A. J. Adderley, Esq., C.M.G.
T	BRITISH HONDURAS	A. J. Adderley, Esq., C.M.G.
U	WEST AFRICAN COLONIES	Sir James Marshall.
V	MALTA	Sir V. Houlton, G.C.M.G.
W	CYPRUS	Hamilton Lang, Esq.
X	FALKLAND ISLANDS	The Secretary to the Royal Commission.

Z INDIAN EMPIRE.
The Secretary to the Royal Commission.

Refreshments

May, 1886.

Wilson Bennison, Surveyor to the Royal Commission.

INTERNATIONAL EXHIBITION
(COPYRIGHT)

1-ROYAL ALBERT HALL. SOUTH SIDE.

Six concerts a week were put on by Novello, Ewer and Company from November 1874. Monday was ballad night, Tuesday English music, Wednesday classical music, Thursday oratorio, Friday Wagner and Saturday popular night. The concerts were not a commercial success and were reduced to two a week.

Above, and below left The contralto
Clara Butt, a former pupil of the
Royal College of Music, was one of
the most popular singers at the Hall
and had been a favourite of Queen
Victoria. She often appeared with
her husband, the baritone Robert
Kennerley Rumford, who disliked
her singing romantic songs with
anyone else.

Top left Adelina Patti, who was the
world's highest-paid singer, drew
crowds to the Hall for two decades.

Far left The Australian soprano
Dame Nellie Melba made her
London debut in 1888 and appeared
at the Hall a score of times between
1911 and 1926.

PROFESSOR HORNE'S BOYS.

"WELL DONE"

THE ÆSTHETIC SMASHER.

G.P.O.

A PRETTY FINISH

"EXCELLENT"

WRESTLING

FIRE ESCAPE EXERCISE SAVING LIFE FROM A SUPPOSED FIRE.

ARRIVAL & DEPARTURE OF CAP. ANSTRUTHERS BAA LAMB

STAFF SERGEANTS CAPPER & WILKINS DOUBLE SOMERSAULT

GORBOULD

A Hard Worker for the Tombola

This way to Supper

Policeman. X

Opposite A Grand Military Assault in aid of the Egyptian War Fund in 1883. These events were the basis for accepting sports into the Hall.

Left Costumed revellers at a ball given by the Savage Club in July 1883 in aid of the Royal College of Music. Many went to great lengths to look like authentic Native Americans and dancing went on until dawn.

The audience at a patriotic concert in aid of the Boer War Fund in January 1900, sponsored by the *Daily Mail*. Bands from all over Britain took part and the event 'proved a tremendous success'. That same year the organiser, John Henry Iles (*inset*), brought the National Brass Bands Championships to the Hall.

Overleaf An early photograph of the Hall and Kensington Gore. Just beyond it are Albert Hall Mansions and Lowther House, later the Royal Geographical Society's headquarters, both designed by Norman Shaw.

The 'Truth Annual Toy Show' took place each Christmas for a number of years, organised by the weekly society newspaper, *Truth*. Around 27,000 home-made and other toys were displayed and sold, and each year around 4,000 readers would compete for the 'best-dressed doll'.

Overleaf Part of the terracotta frieze
that encircles the building. Seven
artists were involved in the design,
carried out by students of the South
Kensington Museum, which was
to become the V&A. This section,
depicting 'Architecture', is by the
popular Victorian genre painter
W.F. Yeames.

1901-
1940

Society balls and boxing matches

Albert and Victoria's son 'Bertie' (Edward VII) had a rather different outlook on life. During his reign the Royal Albert Hall became the venue of some spectacular balls and charity occasions. It was also kept in the headlines as a place for sporting events, political meetings and lively debates, especially in the matter of votes for women. In music, Britain could at last be proud of composers of world renown. Edward Elgar and Hubert Parry provided inspirational music during the First World War. Just as popular were the post-war summer choral performances of Coleridge-Taylor's Hiawatha, *conducted by the young Dr Malcom Sargent*

One of the greatest crowd-pleasers of the Edwardian age was the "Russian Lion", George Hackenschmidt, whose appearance at wrestling matches could cause London traffic to come to a standstill. The popularity of this 16-stone gentle giant, who won all his 3,000 encounters, can be attributed to his agent, Sir Charles ("C.B.") Cochran, who from 1926 to 1938 was General Manager of the Royal Albert Hall. It was Cochran who persuaded Hackenschmidt to give the crowd their money's worth by not dispatching opponents too quickly. On July 2, 1904, in a demonstration of "Physical Cultural Entertainment" at the Hall, Hackenschmidt met and bested the American champion Tom Jenkins for a purse of £2,500.

Wrestling was not what one might have expected in Prince Albert's Hall, and it had only been allowed under a number of conditions, one of which was that no boxing should take place. By this time the Marquess of Queensberry had given the sport some respectability with new rules that brought in gloves and restricted amateur fights to three two-minute rounds. Friendly fights had been performed in the Hall as part of military combat displays, and the sport was gaining popularity around the country, in part through the muscular Christianity of the day and also because churches and charitable organisations found it a useful recruiting tool. Easier to organise than team sports, it was also taken up by the new polytechnics.

But some murderous prize fights were within recent memory and among those who remained firmly against the sport was Queen Victoria's successor, Edward VII, whose voice still counted at his father's Central Hall for the Arts and Sciences. In France, Baron de Coubertin, the aristocratic founder of the Olympics, regarded it as something "practised only by the dregs of the population" and it was therefore excluded from the first Olympic Games, in Athens and Paris. The Americans chose the sport for the 1904 Games in St Louis, but it was excluded again in 1912 in Stockholm, where the sport was illegal.

In 1908 the Olympics should have taken place in Rome, but the Messina earthquake intervened and it was transferred to London. A 70,000-seat stadium was hastily built down the road from the Royal Albert Hall in Shepherd's Bush, where the Franco-British Exhibition happened to be in progress, and the Amateur Boxing Association approached the Hall for possible use in October, when the bouts, in five weights, were scheduled. This time the Hall did not object, but in the end the Northampton Institute in Clerkenwell, now City University, was chosen. The Americans were not entered, no Continentals survived the first round and all five gold medals went to the British, raising the sport's profile and popularity. It was not long afterwards that boxing began its long-running relationship with the Hall, which had the advantage of an organ that could be relied on to drown

out disagreements with the referee. Eventually the fights even attracted royalty: both the next two Princes of Wales took ringside seats.

The most dramatic moment during London's IV Summer Olympic Games was when Dorando Pietri from Italy entered the Shepherd's Bush stadium at the end of the marathon begun at Windsor Castle "looking dazed, bewildered, hardly conscious in red shorts and white vest, his hair white with dust", according to *The Times*. He staggered and was helped to his feet several times by, among others, Sherlock Holmes's creator Sir Arthur Conan Doyle, who was a special correspondent for the *Daily Mail*. "No Roman of prime ever has borne himself better," Conan Doyle declared. "The great breed is not yet extinct." The assistance led to Dorando's disqualification, however, and the gold medal went to the next man on to the track, Johnny Hayes of America. The race was shown on Pathé News and dramatically pictured in weekly papers, making Pietri an international hero, and he returned the following December to re-run the event at the Royal Albert Hall. Pietri's competitor this time was a single runner, the best Britain had to offer, C.W. Gardiner. Ninety yards of coconut matting encircled the arena, necessitating 524 laps. If the original race had been disappointing, this one was a washout: thirty-eight laps from the finish, Pietri retired, claiming that he had problems with his shoes.

Baptisms and Banquets
At the start of the 19th century, sport was not far removed from religion. Calisthenics and marching exercises were performed by young women as well as young men to show how healthy they were in both body and soul. The Hall had been given a licence as a place for public worship and religious organisations took advantage of its space. Most memorable of these was the Salvation Army, whose founder, General William Booth, rallied his troops in between his exhausting world and country-wide tours, even appearing on stage with a cheery "toot-toot" from the horn of his white A.C. motor. The Massed Salvation Army Bands came, too, on one occasion sending George Bernard Shaw "out of my senses with enthusiasm". The Sally Army first used the Hall in 1895 and Booth last appeared a few months before he died in 1912, but the association between Hall and Army has continued to this day.

The Torrey-Alexander Mission was the first evangelical movement to arrive at the Hall, hiring it for seven weeks in 1905 and claiming 7,000 converts. Twenty-three years later, Pastor George Jeffreys from Wales led his Elim Evangel of the Four Square Gospel in a mass baptism, creating a "River Jordan" in a large tank. Even Clara Butt used the Hall for religious purposes. In the 1920s, after the death of a son and daughter and the contraction of cancer of the spine, her own faith as a Christian Scientist deepened and she delivered several sermons at the Hall.

All this was a far cry from the gaiety of Edwardian London. Dinners, charity balls and celebrations of Empire were regular events at the Hall throughout Edward's reign. Most balls required fancy dress, and dancing on the purpose-built Great Floor that was erected over the arena and the stalls went on from ten o'clock in the evening until five in the morning. Unfortunately, the King failed to live long enough to see the largest of these events, the Shakespeare Ball of 1911, to raise money for the Shakespeare Memorial Fund. He died while it was in preparation and so it was turned instead into a ball to celebrate the coronation of George V. Sir Edwin Lutyens transformed the Hall into an idyllic, verdant Arden under a brilliant blue sky. Crowds gathered outside to watch the coaches, backed up for half a mile, disgorging their Elizabethan passengers, some of them descendants of the original characters. Photographs and watercolours in a lavish souvenir of the event show all London society and assorted crowned heads in Elizabethan costume. With text by George Bernard Shaw among others, the volume was edited by Sir Winston Churchill's mother, the New Yorker Jennie Jerome, and sold for five guineas. A copy of it might fetch £100 today.

A year before the Shakespeare Ball the Chelsea Arts Club's annual *mardi gras* finally reached the Hall where it settled, via Twelfth Night, into becoming a traditional New Year's Ball held most years until 1958. Before the First World War, it cost three shillings just to be a spectator in the gallery. Though never quite respectable enough to be part of the London Season, the bohemian Chelsea Arts Balls developed a certain reputation and tickets became increasingly sought after. These were not polite events where you hoped to be introduced to somebody eligible. This is where you went to dance with exotic strangers. Each year there was a theme and artists and students from Chelsea Polytechnic as well as the Royal College of Art, then in Exhibition Road, outdid each other for costumes and on the odd occasion dispensed with costumes altogether. The floats were made by the celebrated artists of the day, including Sir Alfred Munnings, and some were so enormous it is hard to know how they got into the Hall at all.

The Song of Hiawatha
The first major charity ball at the Hall that Edward VII attended as Prince of Wales had been given by the Savage Club in 1883 in aid of the Royal College of Music. It was a magnificent affair and guests went to great lengths to dress up as authentically savage Native Americans, even seeking real scalps. The American West was then a place of thrilling adventure exemplified by Wild Bill Hickock who that year began touring with his Wild West Show. But by the end of the century the Native Americans had

been vanquished, their population dramatically reduced, and they were seen in a more sympathetic light. The idea of the Red Indian as a wise and sensitive figure at one with nature had been encapsulated in Henry Wadsworth Longfellow's poem *The Song of Hiawatha*, written in 1855 and still selling in vast numbers. The easy metre of Longfellow's verse made it a natural choice for librettos, and both Sir Arthur Sullivan and Sir Edward Elgar had set his poems to music. In America, Dvořák had considered using *Hiawatha*, but in the end it was Samuel Coleridge-Taylor who turned the epic into a highly successful choral work.

Born in London, Coleridge-Taylor had an English mother and a father who was a doctor from Sierra Leone. He made his public debut playing the violin at the age of eight and became a pupil of the Royal College of Music. By the time he conducted the first performance of Hiawatha's Wedding Feast at the age of twenty-three, his talents as a composer had been recognised by Elgar, among others. The *Musical Times* expressed "astonishment at a composer barely out of his teens showing remarkable originality in almost every bar". Coleridge-Taylor went on to complete the *Hiawatha* trilogy with The Death of Minnehaha and Hiawatha's Departure and he was happy to sell the copyright for the music for fifteen guineas. His death in 1912 at the age of forty-six spared him any regrets he may have had when *Hiawatha* became the Hall's longest-running spectacular. The show was put on by the Royal Choral Society, conducted by Sir (then Dr) Malcolm Sargent. Thomas Fairbairn, a wizard of pageantry and stagecraft, used all the tricks in the book. The 12,000 square-foot backdrop of the Hudson Valley was "The largest picture in the world" and gimmicks included a waterfall, snowstorms and a descent into such gloomy darkness that a light had to be fixed to the top of the conductor's baton. Londoners knew when summer had arrived when each evening the tribes gathered from across the city, a thousand singers dressed as Native Americans making their way from their homes to the shores of Gitche Gumee in South Kensington.

Hope and Glory
In 1921 the Royal Albert Hall celebrated its fiftieth birthday. At the celebratory concert every piece of music was home-grown, with the exception of a song from Gounod's *Faust*. This was included as a homage to the part that the Parisian had played in the original concert, in which not one note had been composed by an English-born musician. All that had now changed. Cheltenham-born Gustav Holst, Bradford-born Frederick (Fritz) Delius and Broadheath, Worcester-born Edward Elgar, who all died in 1934, were the first of a new breed of Britons able to hold their own against any oversees rivals, just as Joseph Barnby had predicted. Edward Elgar's *Land of Hope and Glory*,

forever associated with the Hall, seemed like their rallying call. The tune started life as the Pomp and Circumstance March No 1, which took London by storm at Queen's Hall in London on October 26, 1901, conducted by Sir Henry Wood. "The people simply rose and yelled," he recalled. "I had to play it again – with the same result; in fact, they refused to let me go on with the programme. After considerable delay and merely to restore order I played the march a third time. And that, I may say, was the one and only time in the history of the Promenade concerts that such an orchestral item was accorded a double encore."

The words of *Land of Hope and Glory* were written by A.C. Benson, an Eton school master and son of an Archbishop of Canterbury. It became the Coronation Ode, which was played at the enthronement of George V. Clara Butt recorded it in 1912 and just about everyone who owned a gramophone in Britain possessed a record of her stirring performance.

As the man for all great British occasions, Elgar was one of the seven conductors of seven orchestras that formed the Titanic Band Memorial Concert in the Hall on Empire Day 1912, just over a month after the ship went down. Billed as "the greatest professional orchestra ever assembled", it was several hundred strong and included 84 first violins, 73 second violins, 51 cellos and 49 double bases. The programme for the event reproduced photographs of Henry Wallace Hartley and his doomed eight-man band, "The Heroic Musicians of the Titanic who died at their posts like men". The evening ended with everyone singing *Nearer My God to Thee*, the hymn that Hartley and his band had played as the icy Atlantic folded over them.

Wartime and the British Legion

War time blacked out the Royal Albert Hall. As a precaution against air raids, the black cloth that covered the dome for the showing of films screened in the Hall became a permanent night time feature from 1914 to 1918. The only damage came from an unexploded shell that hit the south side of the building. It can only have stiffened the resolve of those attending the "John Bull" and other patriotic concerts. In 1917, to celebrate the United States' entry into the war, the Columbia Gramophone Company sponsored a Special Invitation Concert for "10,000 Wounded Heroes", and many were on stretchers, brought from hospitals by the County of London Motor Volunteers. Each soldier received a gift of a packet of cigarettes and a programme that bore the request: "Will the audience kindly refrain from smoking until after the duet." The duet was *Night Hymn at Sea* sung by Clara Butt and her husband, the baritone Robert Kennerley Rumford, over whom, at six feet two inches, she soared.

The memory of that war, and of all wars since, is evoked in the annual Royal British Legion Festival of Remembrance, held in the Hall each year on the Saturday nearest to Armistice Day, November 11. In fact it was the *Daily Express* who started the tradition in 1927. It was the newspaper's idea to have a veterans' reunion. "There has never been anything like it in the history of reunions," wrote the journalist H.V. Morton. "Ten thousand Englishmen bound by the mightiest memories of our time, met together to sing to the world the songs they sang in Hell." From the Royal Box fluttered the Union flag that had flown on the Menin Gate at Ypres in Belgium, where *The Last Post* is still played by a bugler at eight o'clock every evening. The following year the British Legion organised the Festival of Remembrance; it has become an annual event.

Votes for Women

One patriotic song that inadvertently arose from wartime was William Blake's poem *Jerusalem*, set to music by Sir Hubert Parry, President of the Royal College of Music. An organisation called Fight For Right, which had been established to counter German propaganda, wanted a rousing tune that could be easily sung. Feelings were running high and some considered playing Bach or Beethoven or any other German composer unpatriotic. Parry became uncomfortable with the strident jingoism of Fight For Right and he withdrew the piece not long after it was first performed. The following year, however, he conducted it at the Hall at a Women's Demonstration meeting and he was delighted when it was immediately taken up as the "Women Voters' Hymn".

The women's movement was as central to the politics of the early 20th century as was trade unionism and the new Labour Party, all of which found a platform at the Royal Albert Hall. In 1921 the journalist Hannan Swaffer wrote in the *Sunday Graphic*, "I have sat in the Albert Hall and heard thousands of people sing *The Red Flag* and *The Marseillaise*. Yes, although the Hall was meant as a memorial to royalty I have heard there thousands of English pro-Bolsheviks cheer the Russian Revolution and yell wildly when Lenin's name was mentioned."

Generally these gatherings were without incident, though the suffragettes, who first hired the Hall in 1907, several times interrupted other political meetings; once again Willis's organ came in handy in attempts to restore order. The organ was itself the unwitting instrument of sabotage when a suffragette was one night found hiding in the pipes, waiting to upset the next day's political gathering by proclaiming her message through a collapsible megaphone that she was concealing.

In the meantime there were always events for women whose consciences were not troubled, such as Mr Sandau's "Quest for the Figure Beautiful" held in 1914. One of the first fashion shows in the Hall, the event included "an unprecedented opportunity to see in one beautiful half-hour of dress delight the most beautiful ladies attire ever brought together". There was also a five-minute *causerie* on figure beauty culture by the management of the Sandau Corset Company.

The Great Outdoors Indoors
Willis's organ was extensively restored by Harrison & Harrison between 1926 and 1934 and music across the board remained a mainstay of the Hall. Regular concerts were given by the popular Irish tenor John McCormack; other visitors included Dame Nellie Melba from Australia, Italy's Beniamino Gigli, Russia's Feodor Chaliapin and Sergei Rachmaninov, Germany's Wilhelm Furtwängler and Spain's Pablo Casals, as well as Maurice Chevalier from Paris and Gracie Fields from Rochdale. Throughout the Twenties and Thirties the Hall continued to reflect tastes and fads of the nation in other ways. Health was promoted through gymnastics and movement with music, and through the Women's League of Health and Beauty. There were gatherings of scouts and girls' and boys' – or "lads" – brigades, a National Community Singing Movement, and international folklore festivals. Table Tennis World Championships were held and the pleasures of cycling were celebrated in a well-attended show.

In 1931 the Hillman Wizard was launched in the auditorium and the Ford Motor Company used the Hall for its annual motor shows in the Thirties. In 1932 it featured the V8, the first model off the miraculous new production line in Dagenham in Essex, "the largest in the Old World", employing 15,000 workers. Other vehicles on the floor included vans, tractors, cattle trucks, travelling shops and the 12-cylinder Lincoln limousine. Promotional films were shown and there were bands every evening of the ten-day event.

Those who could not get to the Royal Albert Hall could go to the cinema to see it instead, as it featured in *Excuse My Glove*, a 1936 film about boxing, and in Alfred Hitchcock's 1934 thriller, *The Man Who Knew Too Much*. Emlyn Williams was involved in the script, which concerned the dramatic thwarting of an assassination attempt in the Hall. Leslie Banks, Peter Lorre and Nora Pilbeam were the stars in this British classic which Hitchcock re-made in 1957 with James Stewart and Doris Day.

A Shadow Across Europe
Real life was, however, never far from the Hall. A few months after Hitler came to power in Germany in 1933 there were prayers in the Hall for intercession on behalf of German Jews, and the Labour Party organised a "National Protest Against the Means to Freedom" in order to highlight "the systematic and brutal persecution of the Jewish people". Later the same year Albert Einstein spoke at a meeting of the Refugees Assistance

Fund. Yet Britain was not immune from the politics of the extreme right. Sir Oswald Mosley, leader of the British Union of Fascists, held four meetings with his Blackshirts in the Hall, the first in April 1934. Their headquarters and parade ground were then a mile away, next to the Duke of York Barracks in Chelsea. The fourth meeting was in March 1936, seven months before Mosley was famously prevented from speaking in Cable Street, the heart of London's immigrant Jewish population. By now passions were so aroused that 2,500 police were on duty and no traffic was permitted within half a mile of the Hall. He was not allowed back.

For Britain, there was a bonus from Nazi persecutions: the appearance in London of a number of talented musicians. They included the most popular tenor in Germany and Austria, Richard Tauber. Born in Linz, this composer, conductor and prolific record-maker many times filled the Hall, becoming a British subject in 1941. Following his death seven years later, the Anglo-Austrian Music Society presented a Memorial Concert at the Hall and the Luton Girls' Choir, which had performed with him on many occasions, donated the proceeds of their last joint recording to establish the Richard Tauber Memorial Scholarship Fund. Other immigrants from Nazi Germany and Austria have made a major contribution to music in Britain, including the Amadeus String Quartet and the composer Josef Horovitz.

Political meetings and events to raise consciousness and money continued throughout the Thirties. In 1939 the virtuoso violinist Yehudi (Lord) Menuhin helped to raise £4,000 for the Women's Appeal Committee for the Relief of German and Austrian Jewish Refugees who were being resettled in Palestine, where Menuhin's own parents had met in 1909. He had made his debut at the Hall in 1929 at the age of thirteen and three years later he played the Concerto in B Minor conducted by its composer, Edward Elgar, who was then seventy-five. Menuhin also appeared with his sister, the pianist Hephzibah Menuhin. The family came from New York, but Menuhin continued to have a long association with Britain and eventually he came to live here, becoming a British citizen, a holder of the Order of Merit and a peer. He celebrated his 80th birthday with a concert in 1996, and a memorial concert followed his death in 1999. Of his many appearances, it was his performance with Elgar and their subsequent recording of the Violin Concerto at the new Abbey Road studios that has proved an enduring musical legacy.

Menuhin later said, "Elgar's music and the quality of Englishness he had, that belonging to nature and the lack of brutality was something…I loved and I think I owe him and his music my whole close relationship and good understanding of the English character."

Programme for the 'Happy New Year Ball' on December 31, 1926. It took 100 men three days to build the dance floor for the season's big event.

50   The Royal Albert Hall

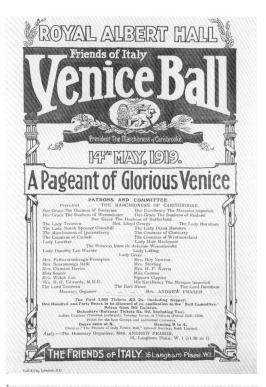

ROYAL ALBERT HALL

Thursday, December 31st, 1925

THE "HAPPY NEW YEAR"
BALL

Among the many charity balls held
in the Hall, the Chelsea Arts Club's
annual costume revel was the best
known and it became a regular
fixture. First held in the Hall in 1910,
it originally celebrated *mardi gras*
(*opposite*) but later moved round to
New Year's Eve where it remained
until its dramatic demise in 1958.

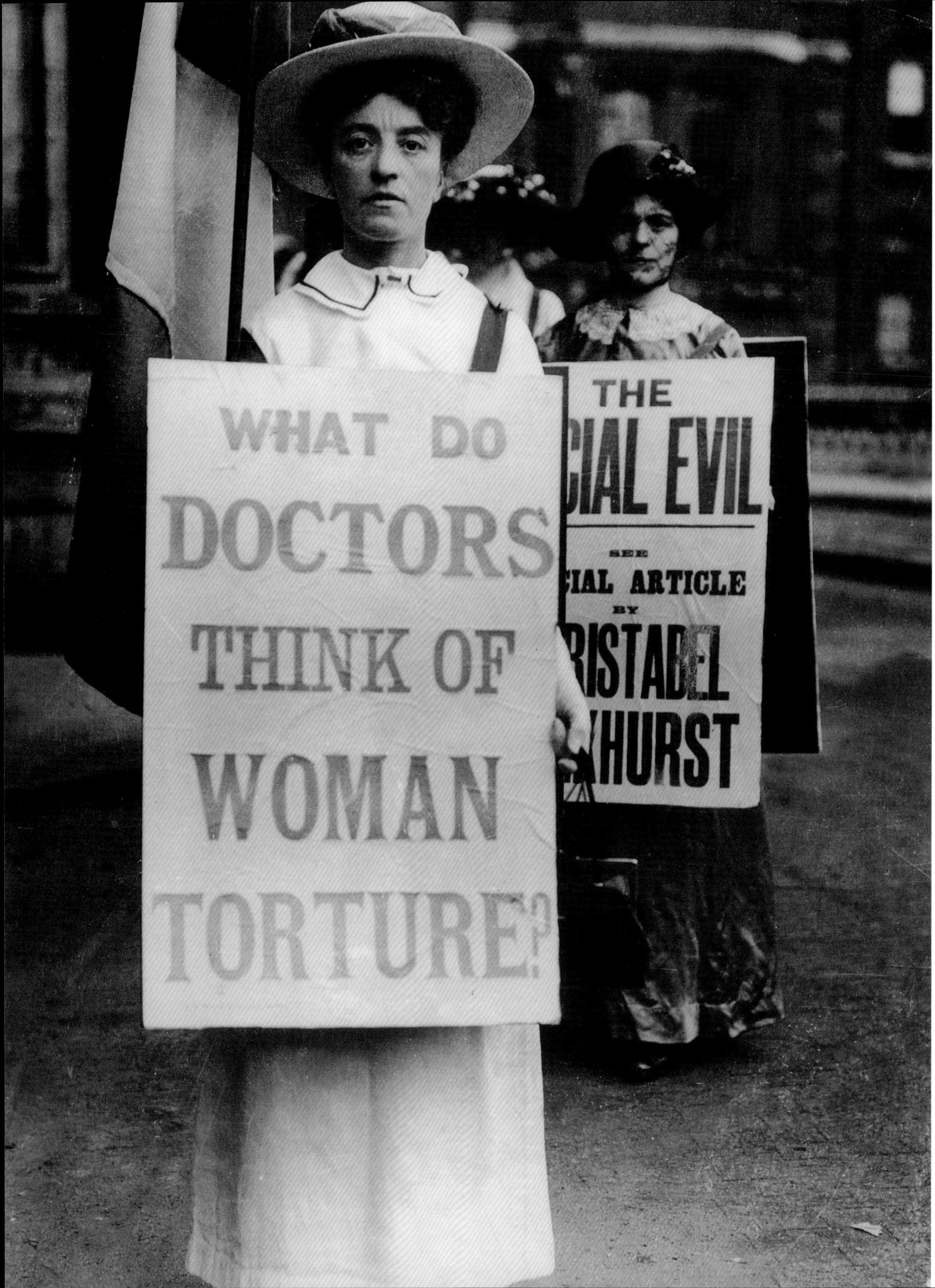
WHAT DO
DOCTORS
THINK OF
WOMAN
TORTURE?
THE
SEE
BY

Left Suffragettes outside the Hall during an International Congress of Medicine in 1908 protest about the force-feeding of hunger strikers.

Above An Irish loyalist meeting in 1893. Although the Council was wary of political events, opinions of every colour were regularly expressed in events at the Hall.

Right When David Lloyd George spoke to a meeting of the Women's Liberal Federation in 1908, Helen Ogston stood up in a box and made a speech, too. Attempts to silence her were met with a dog whip.

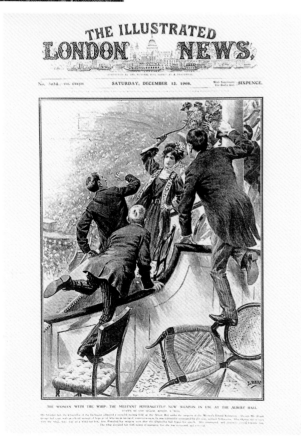

THE ILLUSTRATED
LONDON NEWS.

No. 3634.   VOL. CXXXIII.   SATURDAY, DECEMBER 12, 1908.   SIXPENCE.

THE WOMAN WITH THE WHIP: THE MILITANT SUFFRAGETTES' NEW WEAPON IN USE AT THE ALBERT HALL.

UNDER THE AUSPICES OF THE ORCHESTRAL ASSOCIATION
THE TITANIC BAND MEMORIAL CONCERT
HELD AT
THE ROYAL ALBERT HALL
MAY 24th 1912.

The Philharmonic Society, The Queens Hall Symphony Orchestra, The London Symphony Orchestra, The New Symphony Orchestra, The Beecham Symphony Orchestra, The Royal Opera Orchestra, The London Opera Orchestra and augmented by other members of The Orchestral Association to nearly 500 performers.
THE GREATEST PROFESSIONAL ORCHESTRA EVER ASSEMBLED.

CONDUCTORS

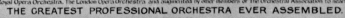

Fritz Ernaldy   Thomas Beecham   Landon Ronald   Sir Edward Elgar.   Sir Henry Wood   Percy Pitt   Wilhem Mengelberg.

Thos. Batty
Chairman of Committee & Treasurer

Hon. Sec.

EXECUTIVE.

EXECUTIVE COMMITTEE			FINANCE COMMITTEE	
Thomas Busby.	E. F. James.	Walter Reynolds.	A. Dyson	J. Edwin Parr
Charles Draper.	F. G. James.	John Saunders.	A. E. Hambleton	W. J. Reynolds.
H. Barwick Evans.	Wilfred James	H. Baldo Warner.	C. W. Hinchcliffe	F. J. Winterbottom
T. H. Gutteridge	C. Bertram Jones	F. J. Waterbottom.	B. Morrow	T. Batty (Treasurer)
E. E. Halfpenny	P. Orcherton.	Ernest A Yonge.		
Claude Hobday	Horace Ralph.	R Fergusson McConnell		
		(Hon Sec)		

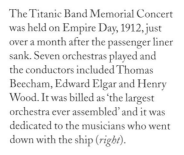

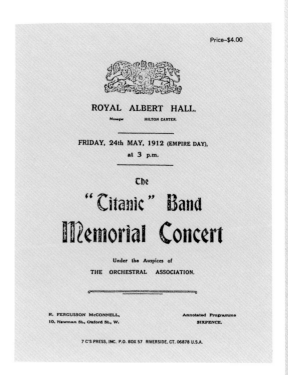

The Titanic Band Memorial Concert was held on Empire Day, 1912, just over a month after the passenger liner sank. Seven orchestras played and the conductors included Thomas Beecham, Edward Elgar and Henry Wood. It was billed as 'the largest orchestra ever assembled' and it was dedicated to the musicians who went down with the ship (*right*).

ROYAL ALBERT HALL

MANAGER ... ... MR. HILTON CARTER

SPECIAL INVITATION CONCERT

TO

10,000 WOUNDED HEROES

(ORGANISED BY MR. LIONEL POWELL)

The following Artists have very graciously given their services

Mme. CLARA BUTT
MARGARET COOPER
AILEEN D'ORME
ADELINE GENÉE
KENNERLEY RUMFORD
GEORGE ROBEY

To Celebrate America's entry into the War, THE COLUMBIA GRAPHOPHONE COMPANY, Ltd., have kindly offered to defray all the expenses connected with this Concert and will present each man with a Souvenir Programme and Packet of Cigarettes

June 24th, 1917, at 3.15

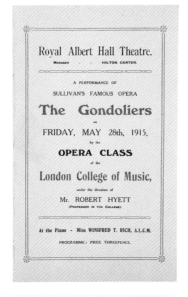

Royal Albert Hall Theatre.

MANAGER . . HILTON CARTER.

A PERFORMANCE OF

SULLIVAN'S FAMOUS OPERA

The Gondoliers

on

FRIDAY, MAY 28th, 1915,

by the

OPERA CLASS

of the

London College of Music,

under the direction of

Mr. ROBERT HYETT

(PROFESSOR IN THE COLLEGE).

At the Piano - Miss WINIFRED T. RICH, A.L.C.M.

PROGRAMME : PRICE THREEPENCE.

 The Grand Priory of
The Order of the Hospital of St. John
of Jerusalem in England.
SOVEREIGN HEAD AND PATRON:
HIS MAJESTY THE KING.

A GREAT

PATRIOTIC CONCERT

Reproduced by kind permission of the Proprietors of Punch.

The St. John Ambulance Association, which forms part of the Red Cross Organisation of Great Britain, derives its name and traditions from the Order of St. John of Jerusalem (Knights Hospitallers), founded at the time of the Crusades.

1099—1914.

SATURDAY AFTERNOON, OCTOBER 24th, 1914,

At 3 o'clock, at

THE ROYAL ALBERT HALL,

IN AID OF

THE ST. JOHN AMBULANCE DEPARTMENT OF THE ORDER.

Above, and below right Concerts went on throughout the First World War, raising money as well as the roof with patriotic songs.

Above right and right Additional entertainment was provided by The London College of Music who put on Gilbert and Sullivan operas in the Royal Albert Hall Theatre. Above the West Porch in what is now the Elgar Restaurant, the Theatre was to become home to the Central School of Speech and Drama.

London College of Music.

SATURDAY,
MARCH 14th, 1914,
8 P.M.

+ + +

Performance

of Gilbert and Sullivan's Opera

THE

MIKADO

(By permission of R. D'Oyly Carte, Esq.)

By the Students of the

COLLEGE OPERA CLASS

IN THE

Royal Albert Hall Theatre,

Under the Direction of

Mr. ROBERT HYETT,

Professor in the College and Conductor of
the Opera Class.

At the Piano - Mr. WALDEMAR SOMMERFELT
(Professor in the College).

Programme - - Price Threepence.

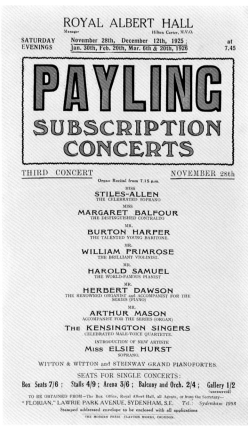

ROYAL ALBERT HALL

ROYAL ALBERT HALL

Manager   Charles B. Cochran.

Sun. MAY 30 AT 3

HAROLD HOLT presents

GIGLI

ONLY APPEARANCE THIS SEASON

At the Piano   -   LUIGI RICCI

BLÜTHNER PIANO   "HIS MASTER'S VOICE" RECORDS

Tickets (inc. tax) Reserved: Stalls 15/-, 10/6, 7/6 Boxes 21/-, 8/6, 6/- (per seat)
Arena 10/6, 6/- Balcony 5/- Lower Orchestra 6/- Unreserved: Orchestra 3/6
Gallery 2/6 from—Box Office Royal Albert Hall, Chappells 50, New Bond Street,
Queen's Hall and usual agents.

Above The Australian contralto Lily
Payling financed regular 'affordable'
concerts between the wars, featuring
gifted young artists as well as
established figures, including herself.

Top Sir Thomas Beecham conducted
in the Hall for more than half a
century. This picture from a 1926
concert programme captures his
dramatic approach.

Left The Italian tenor, Beniamino
Gigli, was one of the world's great
singers to come to the Hall, appearing
from the 1930s to the 1950s.

ROYAL ALBERT HALL

HILTON CARTER, Manager.

Third Concert, Wednesday Evening, May 13th, at 8.30.

Third Appearance in England of

WILLY FERRERO AGED $7\frac{1}{2}$ YEARS

The Youngest Symphony Conductor in the World
who has recently conducted the IMPERIAL ORCHESTRA before
H.I.M. the Czar of Russia, H.I.M. the Empress
Maria Federovna, and the Imperial Court.

The net proceeds of these Concerts
will be given to the Children's
Hospital, Great Ormond Street,
and other charities.

*Analytical Programme
by F. Gilbert Webb.*
Price SIXPENCE.

Right From Turin came the child prodigy Willy Ferrero. He could not read music and conducted from memory. His appearance at the Hall in 1914 at the age of seven brought critical acclaim and he went on to compose music for Italian films.

Opposite 'The Last Appearance' of Adelina Patti in 1906. She returned again, however, in 1914 at the age of seventy-one, for a patriotic concert. In his diary King George V noted, 'Patti sang, wonderfully still'.

The Hall in the 1920s, with a choice of the world's top artistes displayed on posters. The soot and grime of London was beginning to lay a grey mantle over the building.

Posters:
SUNDAY CONCERTS. ...ACHMAN...
SUNDAY CONCERTS. SEASON 1924-5 OCT.-JUNE TETRAZZINI
SUNDAY CONCERTS SEASON 1924-5 OCT.-JUNE LIONEL POWELL & HOLT, 6 CORK ST. W.
SUNDAY CONCERTS. HEIFETZ LIONEL POWELL & HOLT, 6 CORK ST. W.
SUNDAY CONCERTS. SEASON 1924-5 ... OCT.-JUNE. DAME CLARA BUTT LIONEL POWELL & HOLT. 6 CORK ST. W.

BRITISH MEDICAL AS
July 28th, 1932.
Guest of Honour :
Chairman : The Right Hon. LORD DAWSO

CENTENARY DINNER,
bert Hall, London.
CE OF WALES.
.C.V.O., K.C.B., D.C.L., LL.D., P.R.C.P.

Members of The British Medical
Association sit down to dinner
in 1932. The floor was built over the
stalls. Professional bodies, such as
the Institute of Directors, continue
to hire the Hall, which remains
London's largest dining-room.

Os-Ke-Non-Ton (*seated left*), a real Mohawk chief from Canada, played the Medicine Man in *Hiawatha*, the Hall's long-running summer show. It was performed by the Royal Choral Society and dramatic effects included a waterfall and a snow blizzard during which the Hall became so dark that the conductor had to have a light installed on the tip of his baton.

HIAWATHA
ROYAL ALBERT HALL
June 7 19   1937

Souvenir

HIAWATHA
ROYAL ALBERT HALL
JUNE 2-26   1923

Henry Wadsworth Longfellow's
epic poem set to music by Samuel
Coleridge-Taylor was ideal material
for a spectacular event and the
souvenir programmes were always
lavish. *Hiawatha* was staged by
Thomas Fairbairn, a master of
pageants who put on other
entertainments, such as scenes from
Gounod's *Faust* (*above right*).

Left Ford held its annual motor show at the Hall, starting in 1928.

Right New cars launched on the Great Floor included the V8, the first car to come off Britain's pioneering automobile-production line at Dagenham in Essex, pictured in the 1932 programme (*above*).

17 ROUNDS BEFORE THE PRINCE OF WALES: HERMAN BEATS WILDE.

PHOTOGRAPHS BY FARRINGDON PHOTO. CO.

"WE HAVE COME TO SEE A GREAT FIGHT, SO I AM NOT GOING TO MAKE A SPEECH": THE PRINCE OF WALES (WITH CIGAR) AMONG THE SPECTATORS OF THE HERMAN-WILDE BOXING MATCH AT THE ALBERT HALL.

AT CLOSE QUARTERS: JIMMY WILDE (LEFT) AND PETE HERMAN.

THE VICTOR ON THE DEFENSIVE: HERMAN (LEFT) COVERING UP.

THE LOSER ON THE DEFENSIVE: WILDE (RIGHT) COVERING UP.

JUST BEFORE THE REFEREE STOPPED THE FIGHT: WILDE DOWN.

Jimmy Wilde, the popular little Welsh boxer, put up a splendid fight against superior weight when Pete Herman, an American, defeated him at the Albert Hall on January 13. The Prince of Wales was present and received a wonderful ovation. When the cheers died down, he said: "We have come to see a great fight, so I am not going to make a speech. I am sure we wish the men the very best of luck." He then shook hands with them. The fight continued till the seventeenth of the twenty rounds arranged. Wilde then received a hard right and fell through the ropes. He rose and was knocked down again, whereupon the referee, Mr. Smith, stopped the contest. When weighed just before it began, Herman was 1½ lb. over the regulation bantam-weight (8 st. 6 lb.), so Wilde claims to be still Bantam-Weight Champion of the World. In the afternoon Herman had been within the required limit. Wilde said afterwards that Herman was the cleanest American fighter he had met, and Herman spoke of the sporting welcome he had received from the British public.

Above King George V and Queen Mary with the Princess Royal in the Royal Box for a 1934 concert in aid of the Musicians' Benevolent Fund.

Right Queen Mary was an inveterate concert-goer. Here an RAH steward salutes her as she leaves a children's Coronation tea party in May 1937.

Left In 1921 the Prince of Wales witnessed the defeat of the Welsh bantam-weight Jimmy Wilde by Pete Herman of the USA in seventeen rounds.

Above Oswald Mosley rallying his fascist Blackshirts. At his last meeting in 1936 2,500 police were on duty and no vehicles were allowed within half a mile of the Hall.

Right The Prime Minister, Stanley Baldwin, addressing a meeting of the Women's Unionist Organisation in 1930. On his left is Gwendolen Guinness, Countess of Iveagh, chair of the organisation and Conservative MP for Southend-on-Sea.

Albert Einstein speaking at a meeting
to raise money for the Refugees
Assistance Fund in October 1933.
The turbulence in Europe caused by
Hitler's rise to power earlier that year
resulted in a number of meetings at
the Hall.

Queen's Hall near Broadcasting
House on the morning of May 11,
1941. Its destruction left the Henry
Wood Promenade Concerts
without a home.

From Proms to pop concerts

Henry Wood's Proms, which had taken place in Queen's Hall near Broadcasting House for nearly half a century, came to an abrupt halt on the night of May 10–11, 1941. The war's most ferocious bombing raid on London completely destroyed the building. To continue the annual promenade concert series, Wood and the BBC turned to the Royal Albert Hall where, under Malcolm Sargent and a host of famous conductors, the biggest festival of music in the world grew and expanded. Popular music crept into the Hall, too, with jazz and pop concerts, and the Beatles and the Stones appeared on the same bill. The spotlight also fell on Eurovison Song contestants and Miss World

A blue plaque on the face of Albert Hall Mansions opposite the east entrance of the Royal Albert Hall reads, "Sir Malcolm Sargent (1895-1967) lived and died in a flat in this building". Overlooking the park and seventy-five brisk steps from the artists' entrance to the Hall, his flat was ideally situated. The building was designed by Richard Norman Shaw in 1879 as one of the earlier blocks of flats in London. Norman Shaw also designed the magnificent private residence of the Hon William Lowther, MP, and his artist wife, Alice, on the east side of the Mansions, which in due course was taken over by the Royal Geographical Society.

No 9 Albert Hall Mansions was on two floors with a staircase that rose towards a stained-glass skylight. There was enough space for an office, a grand piano in the music room, a butler's quarters and a succession of budgerigars, all called Hughie. It was found for Sargent by Lady Mountbatten just after the war. Furniture, from carpets to cutlery, came from Broadlands, Edwina Mountbatten's family home in Hampshire, and it stayed there for the rest of his life. All that the Hall's most famous conductor needed to add was his library of music scores.

Henry Wood's Proms
Sargent had met Edwina Mountbatten around the time that he was conducting the London Philharmonic Orchestra in a ten-city "Blitz tour" of Britain, during which his own Kensington home was destroyed. Music venues, like all places of entertainment, opened when they could during the bombing, which had begun during the Henry Wood Promenade Concert season at Queen's Hall in 1940. At this time all London was at the mercy of air raids and when bombs shattered some of the glass in the roof and windows of the Royal Albert Hall that autumn, it closed down. It did not open again until the end of May the following year when concerts and meetings continued, including hush-hush briefings by government officials.

On the afternoon of May 10, 1941, a few weeks before the Hall re-opened, Malcolm Sargent was at Queen's Hall conducting the Royal Choral Society in Elgar's *The Dream of Gerontius*, with Webster Booth among the soloists. That night the worst air raid of the war began. For five hours under a fatally bright moon more than five hundred Luftwaffe bombers spread incendiary devices and high explosives across the city leaving 1,436 dead and 1,792 injured. The House of Commons, the House of Lords, Westminster Abbey, the British Museum, the Mint, Mansion House, St James's Palace, and the Tower of London were all hit. Queen's Hall was completely destroyed.

When the Royal Albert Hall re-opened it was the remaining large concert hall in the capital and so it became home of the annual Henry Wood Promenade Concerts. These had been broadcast on the wireless since 1927 and the rituals of the series that took place every August and September were firmly established. Wood conducted the BBC Symphony Orchestra in a variety of works, but maintained a tradition on the Last Night, when he arrived in a coat and scarf, carrying a hat, apparently impatient to leave, and urging on the orchestra with increasing fervour, rushing with break-neck speed through the Hornpipe from his *Fantasia on British Seasongs* to tumultuous cheers.

With a large arena and exceptional gallery, the Royal Albert Hall was eminently suitable for concerts at which the audience could promenade. Less intimate than the 2,500-seat Queen's Hall, it nevertheless filled up for the 1941 Proms. The BBC Symphony Orchestra had decamped for the country at the start of the war, and their place was taken by the Royal Philharmonic and London Symphony Orchestras. The following year, however, the BBC returned to take over the management of the Proms, and among new works was Shostakovich's Leningrad Symphony, which was dedicated to the city then under siege.

Wood was taken ill during the 1943 Proms, which continued under Sir Adrian Boult and Basil Cameron, who vowed to keep playing through any air-raid warning. Wood celebrated his seventy-fifth birthday in 1944 with a concert in the Hall. It was also the Proms' Golden Jubilee, but the programme was interrupted by flying bombs and had to be completed at the BBC studios in Bedford. There Wood collapsed after conducting Beethoven's Seventh Symphony and he died shortly afterwards.

'Flash Harry'
It was Henry Wood who had first brought Malcolm Sargent to London. Born 1895 and brought up in Stamford, Lincolnshire, Harold Malcolm Watts Sargent had become the youngest doctor of music in the country while he was organist at Melton Mowbray church. In 1920, a year after receiving his doctorate, he composed and conducted *An Impression on a Windy Day* for the Queen's Hall Orchestra, which was playing at a charity concert at the De Montfort Hall, Leicester. Impressed, Wood invited him to conduct the piece at the Queen's Hall Proms in London the following year. From then on Sargent decided to concentrate solely on conducting and in 1925 he took up the baton for the Royal Choral Society at the Royal Albert Hall.

Sargent was also taken on as assistant conductor of the London Philharmonic Orchestra, founded by Sir Thomas Beecham, Bart, grandson of the inventor of Beechams Pills. Beecham called him "Flash Harry". A slim, dashing figure in chalk-stripe suits, immaculately slicked hair and carnation (red during the day, white in the evening), Sargent had a panache that appealed to both musicians and audiences. During the war he became Britain's "musical ambassador", flying to neutral countries such as

Sweden and Portugal to raise morale. On one of these occasions Sargent encountered Herbert von Karajan and the Berlin Philharmonic, who had been sent to out-do him. On meeting, Karajan, a member of the Nazi party, told him, "When the Führer gets to London, you will be shot." To which Sargent replied, "How gratifying to be on the wanted list of the SS." (On January 4, 1973, von Karajan conducted the Berlin Philharmonic in a concert in the Hall to mark Britain's entry into the European Economic Community. It was one of the shortest on record, Beethoven's Fourth and Fifth Symphonies lasting just sixty-five minutes. When patrons remonstrated with him, von Karajan said that he gave quality and not quantity.)

Sargent also became a household name during the war as a quick-witted panellist on The Brain's Trust radio programme. It attracted 13 million listeners and women would queue outside the BBC studios for his autograph. In 1947 Sargent and Lord Olivier, a former pupil of the Central School of Speech and Drama at the Royal Albert Hall, were both in the King's Birthday Honours List. They were the first divorcees to be knighted. That same year Sargent became prinicpal conductor of the Proms and he moved into Albert Hall Mansions. For the first time the Proms were broadcast on television and his fame was assured.

Sargent possessed great energy, and his musicianship and expertise were in constant demand. For the 1951 Festival of Britain, which celebrated the centenary of Prince Albert's Great Exhibition of 1851, he was made a consultant for the new Royal Festival Hall. This was was to be the centrepiece and only lasting building of the Festival. Plans to rebuild Queen's Hall had evaporated and central London desperately needed a major concert venue. This purpose-built hall promised to be the best. For its opening concert Sargent wrote and conducted a new arrangement of Thomas Arne's *Rule Britannia*, which was afterwards regularly played at the Last Night of the Proms, which Sargent conducted for the rest of his life.

Although the arrival of the Proms had confirmed the Hall's place as a major concert venue, it could not be complacent and the imminent arrival of the Royal Festival Hall caused it to look to its laurels. In a major overhaul in 1949, the acoustics were tackled by the removal of the original, dust-laden velarium and the instalation of a fluted aluminium inner roof.

In the 1950s the Proms began broadening their programme, opening their doors to other orchestras. Sir John Barbirolli's Hallé was one of the first to arrive. William Glock, appointed BBC Controller of Music in 1959, determined to widen the net further with contemporary work, guest conductors and orchestras from all over the world. Sir Colin Davis made his first appearance in 1960 conducting Stravinsky's *Oedipus Rex* and in 1963 foreign conductors were included for the first time. Sir Georg Solti

brought the Covent Garden opera with Wagner's *Götterdamerung* and Carlo Maria Giulini conducted Verdi's Requiem. The popularity of the Proms increased and queues of Prommers outside the Hall waiting for tickets, with sleeping bags and picnics, were photographed every summer by the press and shown on television news.

For two decades, Sargent was the face and driving force of the biggest musical festival in the world. His astonishing energy, both at the Hall and on the many tours that made him "Britain's ambassador of music", belied the fact that in his early thirties he had contracted tuberculosis. In 1967, at the age of seventy-two, he was suffering from cancer, and he missed the opening Prom, which was conducted by Colin Davis. Supported by drugs and doctors, he made his way across the road from Albert Hall Mansions for the Last Night. He was unable to conduct but he made a speech, which was watched by millions on television. It was an extraordinary farewell.

Looking East

In the Fifties, the Cold War was warmed by the arrival at the Hall of a number of sensational Soviet and East European acts, brought to Britain by the London impresario and agent Victor Hochhauser and his wife Lilian. Another welcome immigrant from the upheavals in Europe, Hochhauser had come to Britain in 1939. After Stalin's death in 1953 he was able to bring Soviet musicians such as David Oistrakh, Mstislav Rostropovich and Dmitri Shostakovitch to this country.

Yehudi Menuhin, another Hochhauser client, had been the first Western musician to play in the USSR after the war when he accompanied Oistrakh, the Ukranian violinist, in Bach's Double Concerto. Oistrakh's Western debut, courtesy of the Hochhausers, was in 1954 and ten years later he was back, playing at the Hall with Menuhin. There was such a demand for tickets to the concert that free entry was given to the afternoon rehearsals, when a packed Hall watched Oistrakh conduct the Royal Philharmonic Orchestra for Menuhin, and Menuhin conduct for Oistrakh. The following year the violinists returned, with Oistrakh's violinist son, Igor, and the Moscow Philharmonic Orchestra, an event that was televised and seen by millions.

The Hochhausers brought other acts, too. Soon London had been introduced to balalaika players, gypsy ensembles and sundry folk dancers, with such troupes as the Ukranian State Cossack Company, the Georgian State Dance Company, the Dagestan Dance Company, the Soviet Army Ensemble and, in 1960, while the Soviet delegation was walking out of the disarmament talks in Geneva, the Bolshoi Ballet.

The Soviet Embassy, a short walk away in Kensington Palace Gardens, was well placed to keep an eye on proceedings. In 1964 the Moiseyev Dance Company was performing, parodying the West with a pop group meant to look like The Beatles, who had appeared at the Hall for the first time the previous year. Unknown to the Soviet ambassador, Paul McCartney had taken a seat in the box alongside his, to see it for himself.

It was impossible, however, to keep politics out of culture, and when the Soviet army crushed Dubcek's reform movement in Czechoslovakia in the Prague Spring of 1968, an invitation to the Red Army Ensemble to come to the Hall was revoked by the British government. The Soviet invasion was marked by a charity concert held in aid of Czech students with Daniel Barenboim conducting the London Symphony Orchestra and his wife, Jacqueline du Pré, the soloist in Dvořák's Cello Concerto.

By 1974 the Hochhausers' fount of talent had dried up. Vocal "Refuseniks" were being denied exit visas from the Soviet Union, which became more and more concerned about defections to the West. But Rostropovich defected, staying at the Hochhausers' London home. There was no more dealing with the Soviet Ministry of Culture until Gorbachov's *glasnost* of 1989.

Art Students and All That Jazz
Before the war the Royal Albert Hall had never been a venue for big bands or jazz, and its dance floor was used only for charity balls. But in the 1950s popular music and ballroom dancing arrived. In 1958 the *New Musical Express* held its annual awards here, compered by Pete Murray who handed Frankie Vaughan the award for the Outstanding British Singer and Voice Personality. Other winners were Marty Wilde, Eddie Calvert, Lonnie Donegan, Cliff Richard, Alma Cogan and Petula Clark. An optimistic request to the US Army in Germany, to ask if its most famous recruit could attend, allowed the *NME* to run the headline "Elvis may receive awards – in person!" Sadly, he never appeared in the Hall.

The following year there were Jazz Saturdays organised by the BBC, and a more adventurous all night "carnival of jazz" with Alex Walsh's Jazz Band. Few of the audience were over twenty, the papers reported. Beards, bowler hats and the granddad look were "the thing" for boys; Little Nell skirts, potato-sack dresses and bloomers made from Union flags for the girls. "By four they settled down to a communal necking session among the Victorian splendour of the Albert Hall" was the caption to a picture of a couple thoroughly embraced on the floor.

The Chelsea Arts Club Ball, meanwhile, was going from strength to strength. In 1957 designs by the tuba-playing cartoonist Gerard Hoffnung included a huge inflatable Malcolm Sargent. "I always associate him with the Albert Hall," he said. "I thought that not to have him floating around would be a discourtesy." The following year there was a sixty-foot figure of the artist Augustus John, the "King of Chelsea", then aged eighty, with designs by Feliks Topolski. This was to be the final occasion. It started out as one of the most uneventful New Year's Eve celebrations largely because the floats, which were usually broken up in a tremendous battle at midnight, were spirited away. "For the first time in its fifty years [in fact forty-eight years], the Arts Ball had not a single free fight as the New Year was ushered in," reported the *News Chronicle*. "Not one fist was shaken in anger." That was in the early editions of the paper. Later editions caught the real story of the 1958 ball. At two in the morning a young man walked on to the dance floor and set off a smoke bomb that "shocked, choked and blinded the thousands of revellers". That was the last of the Chelsea Arts Club Balls at the Hall.

The Sixties
"We were all in our smart new clothes with the rolled collars, and we looked at each other and we were all thinking, 'This is it! London! The Albert Hall!' We felt like gods." Paul McCartney and The Beatles had arrived, as he told his biographer, Barry Miles, and soon they would inform everyone on their *Sergeant Pepper* album that they knew how many holes it took to fill the Albert Hall.

They weren't the only ones who wanted to be stars of the Hall. According to The Rolling Stones' biographer, Philip Norman, after The Beatles' first appearance at the Hall in "Swinging Sound 63", Brian Jones was giving their road managers a hand with equipment, when some girls mistook the "mop"-haired Stone for a Beatle and excitedly rushed over to ask for his autograph. The Stones' manager, Georgio Gomelsky, later recalled, "As we walked away from the Albert Hall, down the big steps at the back, Brian was almost in a daze. 'That's what I want, Giorgio,' he kept saying. 'That's what I want.'" He got it. In September that year the Stones were on the same bill as the Beatles, the only time that the two most famous groups in the history of British pop music ever appeared on the same programme together.

Pop music was now in the air, and the Pop Proms, organised by the burgeoning music papers, were held for several years, but it was two other events at the Royal Albert Hall that have drifted into the hazy myths of the Sixties to become legend. The first was "Gathering of the Tribes", a poetry reading with Allen Ginsberg and nineteen other poets, including Robert Graves and Adrian Mitchell, in June 1965, shortly after American combat troops had landed in Vietnam. According to the opening words of a documentary about the event made by the BBC thirty-five years later, "On this summer night a youth culture found its voice in Britain and the Sixties burst into life." Ginsberg had arrived after being thrown out of Czechoslovakia where he had discovered thousands of fans, and he was staying in London with Barry Miles who recalls the Royal Albert Hall event in his autobiographical book *In the Sixties*: "There was a unique, high-intensity energy in the Hall, caused not so much by the poetry as by the audience; the gathering together of a new generation, a new constituency of youth, not yet distinguished by dress or length of hair, but a new community of spirit that was soon to manifest itself, seeing each other for the first time en masse." The boxes were turned into private parties, the poems expressed anger about Vietnam, and some performers, including Ginsberg, became progressively drunk. One girl stood throughout it all, dancing and waving her arms as if in a trance. It was all a sign of things to come.

The next historic event in the milieu of pop culture was the arrival of Bob Dylan on the last stop of his 1966 world tour with The Band, then called The Hawks. They had two dates at the Royal Albert Hall: May 26, when The Rolling Stones were in the audience, and May 27, when The Beatles were watching. A sound engineer recalled seeing Dylan talking to a fire extinguisher just before the concert, and he was convinced that the singer was so "out of it" that he would not appear. George Harrison knew what Dylan was going through. "I felt a bit sad for him because he was a bit wasted at the time," he said. "He'd been on a world tour and he looked as if he had been on a world tour. He looked like he needed a rest."

In the event the performances were perhaps the best of the tour, which was seminal in rock music history, bonding folk for the first time with rock and roll. In the first half Dylan played his usual folk-protest-style tunes. In the second the band let rip with ear-splitting electronic music that all but drowned out the howls of protest from the folk fans in the audience. One of them called out "Judas!" and Dylan called him a liar and told the band to play louder. All this is recorded on *Live 1966 – The Royal Albert Hall Recordings*. The only trouble with it is that these recordings, for thirty years available only as a bootleg album, turn out not to have been made at the Royal Albert Hall. In 1996, when Columbia released the official CD, it became clear that, in spite of the title, all the recordings, including the Judas incident, had in fact taken place in the Free Trade Hall in Manchester where Dylan had played ten days earlier. Whatever the truth is, the Hall is indelibly associated with what has variously been described as "The Holy Grail of Rock and Roll" and "the greatest live rock-and-roll album ever released".

By the end of the Sixties the Hall had firmly established its credentials as a pop venue. Cream's farewell concert took place in November 1968. John and Yoko climbed into a bag during "An Alchemical Wedding", causing a member of the audience, 24-year-old Elizabeth March, to remove all her clothes. Jimmy Hendrix and Janis Joplin had solo concerts, and The Rolling Stones appeared with Ike and Tina Turner . In June 1969 Frank Zappa and the Mothers of Invention took over the Hall for a concert that was recorded as *Uncle Meat*, featuring Don Preston playing *Louie Louie* on "The mighty majestic Albert Hall pipe organ". The ghost of the instrument's maker, "Father" Willis, one of several apparitions that have been reported in the Hall, no doubt roamed restlessly that night.

Global Vision
Among other American performers at the Hall in the post-war era were Duke Ellington and Danny Kaye, who appeared with the London Philharmonic Orchestra for their National Appeal Fund. The orchestra's inexpensive Industrial Series, designed to bring music to workers, eventually became Classics for Pleasure, one of EMI's most successful record series. Other events included a performance from *The Sound of Music*'s original Trapp family singers and a boxing bill with three members of a less wholesome family: the three Krays, twins Ronnie and Reggie and brother Charlie. There were British Nylon fairs and fashion shows, too, one directed by Franco Zeffirelli, plus a visit from the American evangelist Billy Graham at a pageant to celebrate the 350th anniversary of the Pilgrim Fathers' journey to the New World.

The Hall was also selected to stage two major international competitions. In 1968 the Eurovision Song Contest was hosted by Britain for the third time, though it was new to the Royal Albert Hall where it became the first European-wide colour television broadcast. Katie Boyle was the compere and Cliff Richard's *Congratulations* was narrowly beaten by Spain's *La la la* sung by Massiel.

The following year it was the turn of Miss World. The contest, originally called the Festival Bikini Contest, was organised for the Festival of Britain in 1951 by Eric Morley, the public relations director of Mecca Ballrooms. Soon shortened by newspaper headline writers to "Miss World", it became an annual event, although protests from Catholic Spain and Ireland ensured a one-piece was made the order of dress. The annual Miss World contest was held at the Lyceum Ballroom until 1969 when it arrived at the Royal Albert Hall and the following year it was compered by Bob Hope. However, 1970 had been declared The Year of Women's Liberation and feminists had complained that the event was nothing more than a cattle market. When the London-born American comedian came on stage to speak, bags of flour, tomatoes and smoke bombs were hurled towards the stage. Police were called and several arrests were made. Angry at the interruption, Hope said that the protesters must be on "some kind of dope" and went on to confirm their worst fears in his stand-up routine when he said, "It *has* been quite a cattle market. I've been out there checking calves."

Above King George VI, Queen
Elizabeth and Queen Mary
attend a Remembrance Day service
shortly after the end of the war.
The Hammercloth is draped over
the front of the Royal Box.

Right Concerts continued when
they could throughout the war,
though precautions had to be taken.

THE LONDON SYMPHONY ORCHESTRA

Leader: GEORGE STRATTON

Conductor: SIR HENRY WOOD

Associate Conductor: BASIL CAMERON

Saturday, July 12th, to Saturday, August 23rd, 1941, at 6.30 p.m.
Doors open at 6 p.m.

SMOKING PERMITTED
(Except in part of Amphitheatre Stalls reserved for non-smokers)

ABDULLAS FOR CHOICE

NOTICE.

In the event of an Air Raid Warning the Audience is requested to leave the Auditorium
immediately and carry out the instructions of the Stewards and Attendants. Shelter is provided
in the various Corridors, but if any persons should wish to leave the building the nearest
Public Shelters are:— Trenches in Kensington Gardens.
Trenches in Hyde Park, Knightsbridge.
Subway in Exhibition Road.

Above Sir Henry Wood watches the Proms at the Hall from a box in 1943. He was not well enough to conduct.

Left Post-war Prommers from a 1950 programme that lamented the passing of toppers, capes and cloaks.

Right For the first Henry Wood Promenade Concert to be held at the Hall, the progamme from the 1940 Queen's Hall concert was re-used. The BBC Symphony Orchestra had left for the country at the start of the war but returned by the time of the Jubilee season of Promenade Concerts in 1944 (*top right*). This was the last series conducted by Henry Wood (*far right*). Flying bombs caused the Hall to close and the series was concluded at the BBC's Bedford studio where Wood collapsed while conducting Beethoven's Seventh Symphony and shortly after died.

Above right The pianist Myra Hess, who made her Proms debut in 1908, made many wartime appearances.

ROYAL ALBERT HALL
(Manager: REGINALD ASKEW)

THE

ROYAL PHILHARMONIC
SOCIETY

INSTITUTED 1813

UNDER THE IMMEDIATE PATRONAGE OF
HIS MAJESTY THE KING
HER MAJESTY QUEEN MARY
HIS ROYAL HIGHNESS THE DUKE OF KENT
HIS ROYAL HIGHNESS THE DUKE OF CONNAUGHT AND STRATHEARN
HER ROYAL HIGHNESS THE PRINCESS BEATRICE

THE HUNDRED-AND-THIRTIETH SEASON
1941—1942

FOURTH CONCERT   SATURDAY, JANUARY 17th
2.30 p.m.

Solo Pianoforte :
MYRA HESS

Conductor :
SIR ADRIAN BOULT

LONDON PHILHARMONIC ORCHESTRA
(Leader : REGINALD MORLEY)

PROGRAMME   -   -   -   SIXPENCE

SMOKING IS NOT PERMITTED

NOTICE
In the event of an Air Raid Warning the Audience is requested to leave the Auditorium
immediately and carry out the instructions of the Stewards and Attendants. Shelter is provided
in the various Corridors, but if any persons should wish to leave the building the nearest
Public Shelters are :—
Trenches in Kensington Gardens.
Trenches in Hyde Park, Knightsbridge

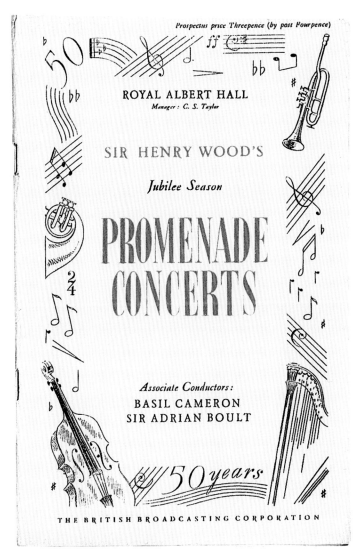

Prospectus price Threepence (by post Fourpence)

ROYAL ALBERT HALL
Manager : C. S. Taylor

SIR HENRY WOOD'S

Jubilee Season

PROMENADE
CONCERTS

Associate Conductors :
BASIL CAMERON
SIR ADRIAN BOULT

50 years

THE BRITISH BROADCASTING CORPORATION

THE ROYAL PHILHARMONIC SOCIETY

PROMENADE
CONCERTS

~~1940~~
1941

SIXPENCE

Rationing out sustenance, a mobile
trolley sells tea and softs drinks to
a Prom queue in the summer of 1948.
In the background is the Royal
College of Music.

ENGLISH FOLK DANCE AND SONG SOCIETY

FOLK DANCE FESTIVAL

ROYAL ALBERT HALL

FRIDAY & SATURDAY 4TH, 5TH JANUARY 1952

AT 7·30 P.M.

SOUVENIR PROGRAMME · 2/-

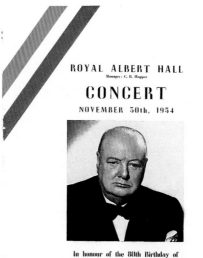

ROYAL ALBERT HALL
Manager: C. R. Hopper

CONCERT

NOVEMBER 30th, 1954

In honour of the 80th Birthday of
The Rt. Hon.

Sir Winston Churchill, K.G.

ROYAL ALBERT HALL
(Manager—CHRISTOPHER HOPPER)

Sunday, November 28th, 1954

WINIFRED ATWELL
LONDON PHILHARMONIC ORCHESTRA
STANFORD ROBINSON

Programme and Notes—One Shilling

LONDON LAUGHS : ALBERT HALL
"I don't think there's much of a fight on, Bill.
I never 'eard of either of 'em"

Above A New Year festival of the English Folk Dance and Song Society. The Society hired the Hall from 1927 until the 1980s.

Above right The wartime leader Sir Winston Churchill is honoured with an 80th birthday concert. He was the first person to give a television broadcast from the Hall, in 1946.

Right The Trinidadian pianist Winifred Atwell was popular for her piano rags, but she was classically trained and played at the Hall with the London Philharmonic Orchestra.

Far right A Lee cartoon in the London *Evening News* sums up the diversity of the Hall's audiences.

Left In 1949 the 12,000-square-foot velarium that had hung beneath the dome since the opening of the Hall was removed, along with an accumulation of dust that took eight vacuum cleaners a day and a half to remove. The velarium was replaced by an aluminium inner canopy.

Above The roof looks out over 'Albertopolis' past the Royal College of Music and Imperial College's Queen's Tower towards the turrets of The Natural History Museum.

Right Water penetration had made the decorative plaster cove work above the gallery unsafe. It was removed in 1949 and not replaced until 2002 as part of the building's restoration programme.

For decades Malcolm Sargent was the name most associated with the Hall, first as conductor of the Royal Choral Society and its annual performances of *Hiawatha*, and from 1950 as chief conductor of the BBC Symphony Orchestra at the Proms (*right*). From 1947, the Last Night was televised (*above*) and 'Flash Harry' became a household figure.

Opposite From just after the war until his death in 1967, Sargent lived in a flat in Albert Hall Mansions just across the road from the artists' entrance. Pictured with him is his long-time secretary and unofficial manager, Sylvia Darley, OBE. A year after his death she founded the Malcolm Sargent Cancer Fund for Children, with annual concerts that continue to this day.

A Hall full of hats. The annual general meetings of the National Federations of Women's Institutes is part of the fabric, as is their singing of *Jerusalem*, which was taken up by the women's suffrage movement when its composer, Hubert Parry, conducted it at one of their meetings in the Hall.

Above George Thalben-Ball, who was appointed curator and organist of the Hall in 1934 after the world's largest instrument had been restored by Harrison & Harrison. Further modifications were made during the fifty-three years he was in the post.

Left Always in fashion. From light reeds to the thunderous Tuba Mirabilis, a vast range of stops are on offer, but the 'Voice of Jupiter' needed constant attention.

Right The Hall's resident cat found a home in the organ, a companion, perhaps, to 'Father' Willis's ghost some claim to have seen in the Hall.

Left Marlene Dietrich sings at an Alamein Reunion concert in 1963. Field Marshal Montgomery, victor of the Battle of Alamein, led the applause for *Lily Marlene*.

Right The great Wagnerian singer Kirsten Flagstad had already retired from opera performances when she made her farewell to London during the 1957 Proms. The concert was to celebrate the fiftieth anniversary of the death of her compatriot Edvard Grieg and she wore full Nordic costume. The editor of this book attended the concert on September 7, as shown in the extract from his diary.

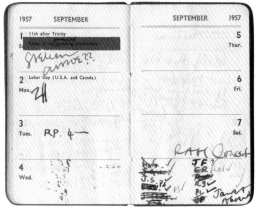

Above James Stewart watches as an assassin falls from a box in *The Man Who Knew Too Much*. Alfred Hitchcock first made the thriller in 1934. This re-make was in 1957 and he is seen here in the Hall (*left*) with Stewart's co-star, Doris Day.

Right An all-night 'carnival of jazz' with the Alex Welsh Jazz Band was held in 1959. By four in the morning some of the audience had descended into 'a communal necking session'.

The Keep Fit Association's Ladies'
Day at the Hall. The Association was
founded in 1956 to promote fitness
through movement, exercise and
dance. Its annual gatherings at the
Hall still bring women from all over
the country.

The Georgian State Dance Company
brought warmth in the Cold War.
In the 1950s a number of traditional
music and dance ensembles from the
Soviet Union and Eastern Europe
came to the Hall. Defections to
the West eventually led to a Soviet
clamp-down on these tours.

Alan Ginsberg reads his poems at the 'Gathering of the Tribes' poetry festival. The event was recorded by the artist Feliks Topolski (*right and overleaf*) who later recalled the 'memorable night on 11 June, 1965, when 3,000 hippies (with thousands more clamouring outisde), stoned and chorally festive, celebrated as never before or since International Poetry'.

TOPOLSKI's CHRONICLE Nos. 5-6 (281-282) Vol. XIII 1965

INTERNATIONAL POETRY AT THE ROYAL ALBERT HALL
LONDON

Pablo Neruda promised but failed to come. He was tracked down at a more formal reading in Belgrave Square. Not all the poems reproduced here were recited at the Albert Hall.

WHAT HAPPENED AT THE ROYAL ALBERT HALL?

Though it came about spontaneously in the best tradition of "happenings", the international poetry presentation at the Royal Albert on the evening of June 11 crystallized out of a very contemporary ferment: that's to say, it was no fluke. It was sudden and perhaps . . . if we are to judge from the level of the production . . . over-hasty; that it took place when it did and not perhaps a few months later and more expertly as part of a wider and more coherent strategy—this is to be explained by a few chance coincidences: the presence of so many foreign poets in London, the happy impulse of two young poets, the availability of the hall, etc. Still, just as we have to look farther than

the Sarajevo murder for the cause of the First World War, so do we have to look beyond these coincidences for the reason behind what happened at the Royal Albert Hall.

One might say it was in the air, has been since after 1945, this felt need on the part of poets, artists, thinking individuals in general for a coming together internationally of individuals in an immediate way, transcending politics. In another place, I called this growing protest and the various calls for some kind of direct action the "invisible insurrection", and I argued that at its most articulate, this (r)evolt is against the whole gamut of traditional response which is unconscious

for the most part, hallowed by convention, and quite inadequate for the complex world which has been thrust upon us by the relentless evolution of our own technology. During the last two decades there have been many international cultural festivals, but this manifestation at the Royal Albert is remarkable in that, conceived, plotted, and undertaken in ten short days, the thousands came and many were turned away at the door.

The impulse to bring all these people together to participate in an evening of poetry was regarded by some of us as a kind of experiment in human festival, a practical demonstration of the immediate availability of creative people of very

different backgrounds to the idea of cultural experiment. And the toleration they showed of some very indifferent poetry during more than four hours was surely evidence of the audience's general appreciation that something was being achieved, something significant and to do with human solidarity, just by our all being there at all in such a place, poets so very different, all together, participating. This concordium was above all a happening, conceived joyfully and seriously in the spirit of play. The idea caught on, the various poets boarded the "shameless bandwaggon" (cf. programme notes), and set about demonstrating that the greatest concert-hall in all England was

hardly big enough to contain all those who, at the shortest notice, would come from all over in answer to this spontaneous gesture of international goodwill. For myself, I think it is not so much a question of choosing to co-operate as of discovering oneself in and of the "invisible insurrection" by virtue of one's practical posture. The (r)evolt is taking place at the level of symbols: there is no question of our ever meeting the forces of reaction head on in a war on their terms. But it is happening. If you are aware of it, you are ipso facto involved. To quote again from the programme notes: "Self-evident for real naked come the words . . ."

ALEXANDER TROCCHI

Disembarked at London Docks

A thin grey figure, tempest or ghosts

the ... of ..., within the:-
...los under eyelids
an electronic bowl, over the dark
a plan in four dimensions
a shadow one, including time
~~........................~~
taking as given
the ... of information ...
                            London
                    1965
... ... for his ...
                         to ...
... ... finish
                   for poets ....

Alexander...   Portlatch. 1966

FOR THE ROYAL ALBERT HALL 11 JUNE 1965

Worldscene! Worldtime! Spacebreaker! Wildship! Starman!
Gemini man dangles white & golden — the world floats
on a gold cord & curves blue white beautiful below him —
Vostok shrieks & prophesies, Mariner's prongs flash —
to the waking of Voskhod Earth sighs, she shakes men loose at last
out, in our time, to be living seeds sent far beyond
even imagination, though imagination is awake — tell
poets of your voyages! Prometheus
unbound Icaros & in gold shell with wings
he launches him up through the ghostly detritus
of gods & dirty empires & dying lands, he screams
he mounts, he cries, he shouts, he shines, he screams
like light never down, his home is in a sun
& he shall be the burning unburned one.
In darkness, Daedalus
unbound Orpheus, the dark lips caked with earth & ...
he kisses open, the cold body he rubs
to a new life — the dream
flutters in a cage of crumbling bars, reviving
& then beginning slowly singing of the stars.

Beginning singing, born to go,
To cut the cord of gold. To get
the man new born to go.

                    EDWIN MORGAN

---

1. TO WHOM IT MAY CONCERN

I was run over by the truth one day.
Ever since the accident I've walked this way
    So stick my legs in plaster
    Tell me lies about Vietnam.

Heard the alarm clock screaming with pain,
Couldn't find myself so I went back to
                        sleep again
    So fill my ears with silver
    Stick my legs in plaster
    Tell me lies about Vietnam.

Every time I shut my eyes, all I see is flames.
Made a marble phone book, carved all the names
    So coat my eyes with butter
    Fill my ears with silver
    Tell me lies about Vietnam.

I smell something burning, hope it's just my brains.
They're only dropping peppermints and daisy-chains
    So stuff my nose with garlic
    Coat my eyes with butter
    Fill my ears with silver
    Stick my legs in plaster
    Tell me lies about Vietnam.

2

Where were you at the time of the crime?
Down by the Cenotaph drinking slime
    So chain my tongue with whisky
    Stuff my nose with garlic
    Coat my eyes with butter
    Fill my ears with silver
    Stick my legs in plaster
    Tell me lies about Vietnam

You put your bombers in, you put your conscience out,
You take the human being and you twist it all about
    So scrub my skin with women
    Chain my tongue with whisky
    Stuff my nose with garlic
    Coat my eyes with butter
    Fill my ears with silver
    Stick my legs in plaster
    Tell me lies about Vietnam.

                    Adrian Mitchell

pain though friction

frau
frfranau
frfrfranauau
frfrfrfrananauau
frfrfrfrfranauauauau
frfrfrfrfrfranauauauauau
frfrfrfrfrfrfranauauauauauau
frfrfrfrfrfrfrfr anauauauauauauau

Ernst
(na)

THE GREAT POP PROM

Presented by
Marilyn Roxy
Valentine

Royal Albert Hall
at 2·15 p m on Sunday
15th September 1963

programme one shilling
in aid of the
Printers Pension
Corporation

THE GREAT POP PROM

THE BEATLES
By kind permission of Brian Epstein

THE BROOK BROTHERS
by kind permission of Peter Walsh, Starlite-Artistes Ltd.

BILLIE DAVIS
by kind permission of Robert Stigwood Associates

SHANE FENTON & THE FENTONES
by kind permission of The Wilson Entertainment Agency Ltd.

ARTISTES ARRANGED IN ALPHABETICAL ORDER

CLINTON FORD
by kind permission of Forrester George Ltd.

THE LORNE GIBSON TRIO
by kind permission of The Wilson Entertainment Agency Ltd.

ARTHUR GREENSLADE & THE GEE-MEN
by kind permission of Bernard Rabin

KENNY LYNCH
by kind permission of The Bernard Delfont Agency

COMPERE: ALAN FREEMAN
by kind permission of Lewis-Joelle Ltd.

SUSAN MAUGHAN
by kind permission of The London Palladium

THE ROLLING STONES
by kind permission of Eric Easton & Andrew Loog Oldham

THE VERNONS GIRLS
by kind permission of Artistes Administration Ltd.

THE VISCOUNTS
by kind permission of Starcast Ltd.

'The Great Pop Prom' held at the Hall in September 1963 was the only time that The Beatles and The Rolling Stones appeared on the same bill, and are pictured here in pages from the programme. The Beatles had made their first appearance at the Hall five months earlier. 'We felt like gods,' Paul McCartney later recalled.

THE ROLLING STONES

On the evening of May 10th, five R 'n B fanatics assembled in a recording studio. The results were: "Come On" and, flipside, "I Wanna Be Loved". The Rolling Stones, formed 11 months ago to dep for a group at The Marquee, London, where they got a wildly enthusiastic reception – had cut their first disc; on May 15th the tapes were played to top Decca executives and a decision was taken to rush release the record on June 7th!

Stone by Stone, here they are :- Mick Jagger, 19 – Lead/Vocal and Harmonica – likes money ; Brian Jones, -19 – Guitar/Vocals and Harmonica – smokes 60 a day; Keith Richard, 19 – Guitar – wants a Thames house-boat; Bill Wyman, 21 – Bass Guitar/Vocals – a Chuck Berry fan, and Charlie Watts – the Beau Brummel of the group – Drums. We're sure you'll give this madly exciting group the same tumultuous hearing they've already had all over London and the Home Counties !

the BEATLES

The original Beatles group of John, Paul and George exploded into the Merseyside scene in 1960. Having made their impression there, they at once took off on the first of 5 brilliant night club seasons in Hamburg. They made Pop history last year when joined by Ringo Starr (drums) their debut deck, "Love Me Do", sold enough copies during its first 48 hours in the shops to soar straight into the National Hit Parade. Not only have they since squeezed 2 Number One winners " Please Please Me" and "From Me To You" into their first six months' of recording ; they've scored a fantastic EP success, too, with "Twist and Shout".

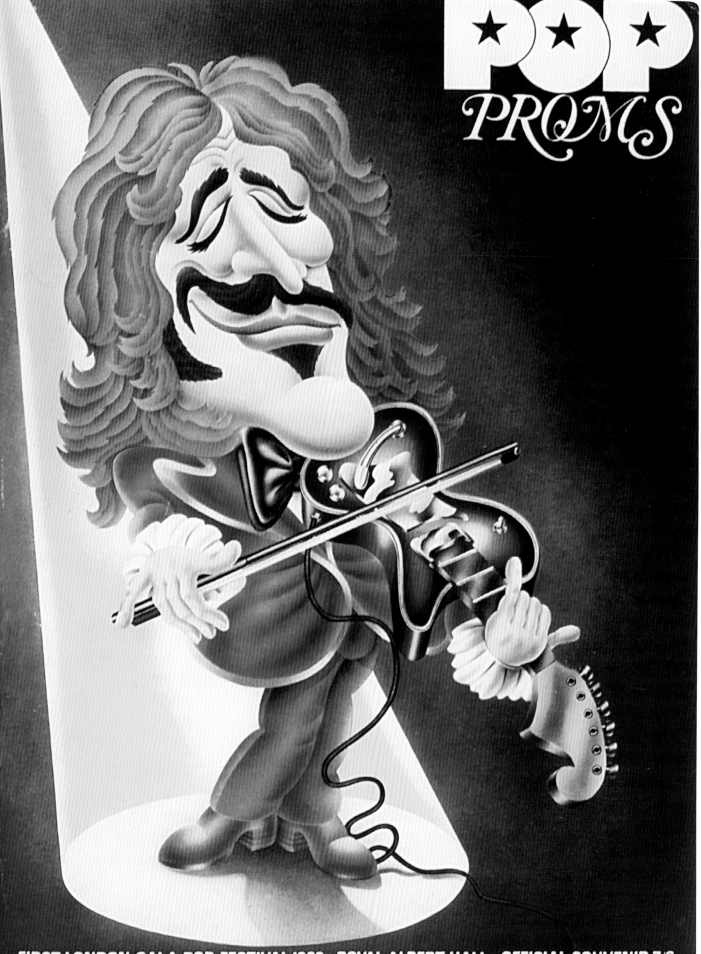

POP PROMS

FIRST LONDON GALA POP FESTIVAL 1969   ROYAL ALBERT HALL   OFFICIAL SOUVENIR 7/6

WITH FULL WEEKS PROGRAMME DETAILS

SOUVENIR BROCHURE TWO SHILLINGS & SIXPENCE

Above Bob Dylan in a programme for one of his appearances in the Hall. His 1966 concert was the last stop on the world tour that produced the seminal *Live at the Albert Hall* CD.

Left Psychedelic guitar hero, Jimi Hendrix, gave a concert in February 1969, a year before his death.

Below The American band, Flock, at a 'Sounds of the Seventies' concert.

Opposite A programme cover for a Pop Proms, designed by Alan Aldridge and Harry Willock.

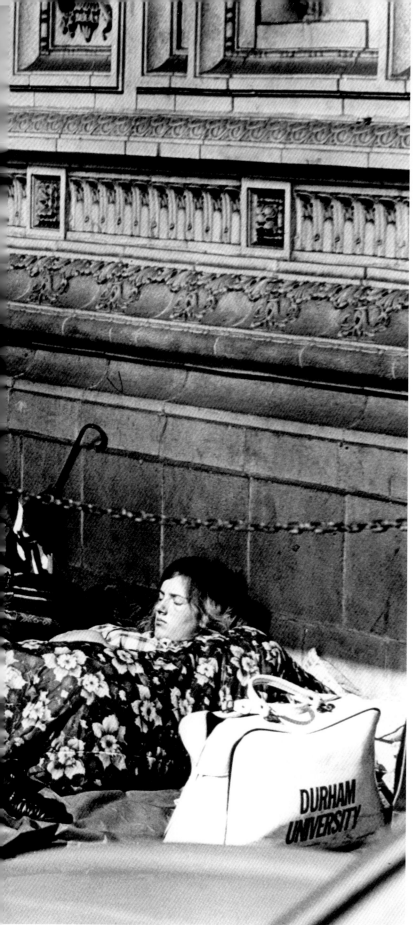

Above Yehudi Menuhin and David Oistrakh gave a concert together in 1962, in which they took it in turns to conduct each other. The concerts quickly sold out, so they gave a free afternoon performance.

Left Prommers settle down on the pavement for a long wait for the best places in the arena and gallery.

Below The Boy Scouts regularly appeared at the Hall. This was their contribution to the 1953 Coronation year, in an event devised by Ralph Reader, who staged around 150 shows and pageants at the Hall, including Festivals of Remembrance.

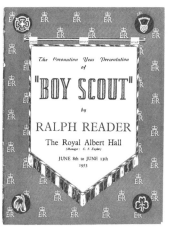

The Coronation Year Presentation of
"BOY SCOUT"
by
RALPH READER
The Royal Albert Hall
(Manager: C. S. Taylor)
JUNE 8th to JUNE 13th
1953

Left Caribbean carnivals organised
by travel companies in the 1980s
offered prize trips for the best festive
costume designs.

Right Twiggy, model turned singer,
gave a solo performance in 1977.

An investigation into the acoustics in 1969 attempted to overcome the echo caused by sound reflection in the dome and its peripheral cove. The result was the installation of 109 glass fibre reflectors measuring between six and twelve feet in diameter. Dubbed 'flying saucers', they were suspended from the ceiling.

Left Technicians check the sound with a reflector microphone, a pistol and a bassoon.

Above The Miss World Contest came to the Hall in 1969 when the crown was bestowed on Eva Rueber-Staier of Austria *(fourth from right)*.

Opposite The following year, the event was hosted by Bob Hope who was attacked by feminists outside and inside the Hall, where flour bombs were thrown. Additional friction was caused by two contestants from apartheid South Africa, one black and one white. The winner was Jennifer Hosten of Grenada.

Overleaf Attending a concert on
March 29, 1971, to commemorate
the centenary of the Hall, Queen
Elizabeth II unveils a plaque in the
main entrance to record the occasion.

THE PLAQUE WAS UNVEILED
ON THE 29TH MARCH 1971 BY
HER MAJESTY THE QUEEN
PATRON OF THE ROYAL ALBERT HALL
AT A CONCERT HELD TO CELEBRATE
THE CENTENARY OF ITS OPENING
ON THE 29TH MARCH 1871 BY
HER MAJESTY QUEEN VICTORIA

Opera, sumo and circuses

As events in the Hall became more elaborate, so the need for a dramatic overhaul seemed more pressing. It wasn't enough just to give it a spring clean. With operas, circuses and other spectaculars making increasing demands, the whole Hall, from glass dome to basement, needed a major redesign. It was going to cost £70 million to do most of the updating, including the excavation of a loading dock and car park beneath the Hall. The setting up of the National Lottery provided a lifeline, as it did for many of London's great institutions. As plans are made to celebrate the completion of eight years' building work in the spring of 2004, and even before the Hall once more resounds to the mighty organ, it is clear that the money has been well spent

Nineteen seventy-one was the centenary year of the Royal Albert Hall and it provided an ideal opportunity for a spring clean. A hundred years of London's soot and grime had by now so blackened its façade that if Queen Victoria had seen it she would have undoubtedly declared it in mourning for Albert, whose own memorial over the road in Kensington Gardens had fallen into a sorry state of decay. The fact was that by the end of the Sixties the Victorian idea of the world was out of favour and nobody was prepared to spend money on a memorial that many regarded as a vanity from the shameful period of Empire.

The Hall, however, was still held in some affection, and it managed to raise £700,000 for a facelift inside and out. A large part of the funds were spent on an abrasive scrub of wet sandblasting which took off the grime and removed messages etched by Prommers hoping for immortality: "Sally and Angela, first in the queue, 1965"; "Phil and Roger from Liverpool, first to queue in 1966". Traditionally the first to stake a pitch makes a list of those who come behind, to prevent queue jumping and to keep a place for people who want to wander off for an occasional break, or pop across the road to the Royal College of Music for a change of clothes for the evening.

Inside the Hall a million visitors a year had taken their toll on the fabric that had faded from a bright blue and ochre to a grubby grey and cream. Sir Hugh and Lady Casson were commissioned for the refurbishment. Margaret Casson was the niece of Francis William Troup, the consultant architect to the Hall in the early 20th century who had pronounced the Great Floor unsuitable for a live elephant that the Chelsea Arts Club had one year wanted to make the star of a New Year ball. As for Sir Hugh (who, ironically, was the architect of the elephant house at London Zoo), he must have had mixed feelings as he saw the grime falling away from the building's façade and the original lustre of red brick and buff-coloured terracotta break through. A former Provost of the neighbouring Royal College of Art, he had been one of the architects associated with its new building on the west side of the Hall a dozen year earlier when the planning authorities had insisted that it was built with soot-coloured materials to remain in keeping with the Hall. Now the modern block looked even more out of place.

Pop Group Ban
This pristine Hall was no place for bad behaviour. The governing Council had been disturbed when The Nice burned the Stars and Stripes on stage, but in the end it was Frank Zappa who put a temporary end to the Hall's rock-and-roll era. The American musical wizard and taboo breaker who had been so free with "Father" Willis's organ on a previous visit, now hired the Hall to perform with his band, the Mothers of Invention, and the Royal Philharmonic Orchestra. The RPO had played on the soundtrack of *200 Motels*, his 1972 movie about life on the road made at Shepperton studios, in which the orchestra also put in an appearance. Now Zappa wanted a live performance. Members of the orchestra had not all been happy with their roles in the movie and there were concerns about the potentially profane and disrespectful lyrics to Zappa's songs, so he was asked to submit a script in advance to the Hall. In defiant response, Zappa described the RPO as "the most ill-behaved bunch of poot-heads" he had ever worked with and refused. The concert was cancelled and all pop groups banned.

Pop groups weren't everything, but they had begun to dominate the music industry and the decision to exclude them from the Hall was bold. The BBC Proms were still – and remain – the biggest classical music festival in the world, but the Hall could no longer rely on classical concerts to fill its engagement diary for the rest of the year. It also faced serious competition. The Royal Festival Hall on the South Bank had been joined by the smaller Queen Elizabeth Hall, seating 1,100, and the Purcell Room for nearly 400. More pressingly, the Barbican Arts Centre, another arts complex arising from the wastelands of the Blitz, was finally nearing completion in the City of London, with a concert hall seating more than 2,000.

Amateur Nights
The Hall continued to be an ideal place for encouraging music. In November 1975 the *Times Educational Supplement* sponsored the first Schools Proms. Four hundred took part and the paper declared: "We knew they would be good. And good they were." It has been an annual fixture ever since.

Another act of faith was "Messiah from Scratch" organised by four academic scientists the previous year. A century after Joseph Barnby had harnessed the voice of London, this quartet of amateur music enthusiasts one day decided to hire the Hall and advertise for ordinary members of the singing public to perform Messiah without rehearsals, just to see what happened. Such spontaneous performance was sound Sixties thinking, which had surfaced the same year with Gavin Bryars's Portsmouth Sinfonia, a band of unrehearsed enthusiasts who set about the Hallelujah chorus with a will and earned themselves the reputation of "the world's worst orchestra". Dr David Burgess, one of the founders of "Music from Scratch", believed that putting on an unrehearsed event was like putting on a party, and if a good performance came out of it, so much the better, but whatever happened everyone should have a good time. Around 2,500 singers and 250 instrumentalists turned up on the night and Gavin Parks, another of the organisers, made his debut as conductor. The occasion was televised, judged a success and became a regular event. Today

"Music from Scratch" is organised by The Really Big Chorus, with three events a year, and for some time it has been associated with the much-revered Sir David Willcocks, a one-time Council member of the Hall and Director of the Bach Choir.

Impromptu scratch performances occasionally occur during the Proms. On some evenings a band of Prommers come together with their instruments for their own amusement outside the Hall. Among them are Hall stewards, often graduates of the Royal College of Music.

Sir Adrian Boult once advised, "If you want to start a career as a conductor, then you start by hiring the Albert Hall." But even those with no intentions of having a musical career have hired the Hall to fulfill a lifetime ambition to stand on the conductor's rostrum and draw recognisable sound from a band of musicians. For inspiration, there has been plenty of choice among the world's great conductors who have appeared at the Hall, from the leaping figure of Leonard Bernstein to mop-haired André Previn, from the high priest Herbert von Karajan to modern Pierre Boulez and meticulous Daniel Barenboim.

Francis Albert Hall

Banning pop groups may have been a financial loss to the Hall, but few of them could fill seats like Francis Albert Sinatra. The generation that scorned Prince Albert also had no time for an old-fashioned crooner and by 1971 he was so out of favour that he went into retirement. But letters from fans begging him to return gave his career an extraordinary second wind. In 1975, on the eve of his sixtieth birthday, he embarked on a world tour with two performances at the Hall. At the end of the tour he placed a full-page advertisement in the *Los Angeles Times*: "It was a very good year. Countries: 8. Cities: 30. Attendance: 483,261. Total performances: 140. Gross $7,817,473."

Staying at his favourite £1,500-a-night suite at the Savoy and seeking out London's top Italian restaurants, Frank Sinatra appeared at the Hall a number of times over the following two decades. Tickets were always at a premium. Feeling quite at home, he would welcome the audience to "Francis Albert Hall", although he was not always at his best. He had autocues to guide him through even his most familiar songs and during the applause for *My Way* he once complained, "I can't stand the song myself." Nevertheless, as Max Bell in *The Times* reported, "It was one of those rare occasions where the Sloanes rub shoulders with the Romfords; where toffs and large, broken-nose gentlemen from the more colourful East End professions are brought together to share a common affection."

In 1989 Sinatra came with Liza Minnelli and Sammy Davis Jr for a concert that was billed as "The Ultimate Event", and his last appearance at the Hall was over six days in May 1992 when he was seventy-six. There would be no more comebacks, he told the packed house, some of whom had paid £350 a ticket, "because I'm not retiring again". At a solo concert in 2001, three years after Sinatra's death, Robbie Williams sung a clutch of his songs, hoping to introduce them to a new generation and duetting with a recording of Sinatra singing *It's Been a Very Good Year*.

Pop's Return

When pop music was allowed back into the Hall in the 1980s, the pause seemed to have coincided with a break in the musicians' own careers and, with some nostalgia, they now took to the stage once more. In September 1983, after a decade of not speaking to each other, The Everly Brothers, Phil and Don, hugged and made up at two Reunion Concerts at the Hall, which were filmed to become a classic pop DVD. They sang twenty-one songs and the audience knew every one of them.

Paul Simon hadn't toured since breaking up with Art Garfunkel in 1982. Five years on, he arrived with the Ladysmith Black Mambazo band in the wake of the success of his *Gracelands* album. There were 100,000 applications for 20,000 seats, and three extra nights had to be added to his appearances. Some believed that the American singer should not have had any dealings at all with apartheid South Africa, but the *Financial Times* reviewer reported, "The concert was like the happiest of summit conferences. If it were left to concerts alone, the peace of South Africa would be secured." The evening ended with a stageful of musicians singing *N'kosi Sikelele Africa*, which resounded around the Hall nine years later in a "celebration of progress in South Africa" as part of Nelson Mandela's state visit.

In 1987 Eric Clapton also made a comeback, after years lost to drink and drugs. He had last played at the Hall in Cream's farewell concert in 1968. Now he came on stage in a shiny blue suit, which the broadcaster John Peel thought made him look like a man collecting betting slips between numbers. "This is from the Sixties," Clapton announced, "if any of you remember them." The audience went wild. Clapton made the Hall the venue of annual concerts for a number of years, and performances from 1990 and 1991 were put together on a CD, *24 Nights: Live from Albert Hall*. He still returns to perform at the venue that he describes as "home".

James Taylor, last seen in the vicinity busking at Hyde Park Corner tube station twenty years earlier, resurfaced in 1988, the same year that the reclusive Canadian Leonard Cohen came by.

Pop musicians' ideas soon expanded to fill the Hall as they began to see it as a place where they could act out their grander pretensions. *The Butterfly Ball* was staged by Deep Purple's Roger Glover in 1975 and *The Hunting of the Snark*, a Mike Batt musical based on a Lewis Carroll story, starred Roger Daltrey and Billy

Connolly in 1987. Daltrey and The Who had paved the way with the "rock opera" *Tommy*, and for many years the band has hosted an annual charity show. These productions were increasingly demanding. Audiences wanted more for their money than a few puffs of smoking dry ice. They were coming to expect lasers and computer-enhanced lighting and effects. One regular spectacular, with angels emerging from the organ and nine real, ermine-clad lords a-leaping, was a Christmas charity fund-raiser, "Joy to the World", which had a ten-year run. The Queen used the first of these events to broadcast her Christmas speech for the first time outside Buckingham Palace, on December 19, 1989.

Sports, Fads and Fashions
Many spectacles required no music at all. Tennis arrived in 1970. Synthetic grass was laid over a special floor erected above the arena and it became a regular venue for a number of tournaments and exhibition matches. First was the Wightman Cup, the annual women's team match played between Britain and the United States and held in each country in alternate years. Britain's single moment of glory in this one-sided affair was in 1978 when Virginia Wade and Sue Barker beat Chris Evert and Pam Shriver. Twenty-five years later Wade returned to play in an anniversary mixed doubles exhibition match. John McEnroe, still going strong in the Honda Challenge, has declared the Hall to be "the most beautiful setting for indoor tennis in the world".

John Curry, the Olympic skating gold medallist described as the "Nureyev of Ice", brought his Art Skating to the Hall in 1984 with "A Symphony on Ice". The arena was frozen over, the Royal Philharmonic Orchestra played and the audience clapped and cheered in all the wrong places. Afterwards the ice was chipped away, put into skips and dumped in the Thames. Eleven years later the Russian All Star Ice Ballet staged "Beauty and the Beast".

Badminton, basketball, squash and karate joined the sporting calendar, and boxing's knock-out occasion was when heavyweight Muhammad Ali fought eight exhibition rounds. In 1991, to show there was always something new under the sun, a sumo wrestling tournament was staged outside Japan for the very first time as part of a nationwide Japanese Festival. Sumo had already become popular on television, and now it appeared in the not inconsiderable flesh. The Hall that had seen the rituals of many faiths, from the baptism of evangelists to the hypnotic whirl of Mevlevi dervishes, now witnessed the *rikishi* combatants scatter salt to purify the *dhoyo*, the platform of compacted clay. Stamping their feet to ward off devils, clapping their hands to get the attention of the gods, these giants balanced on one leg, squatted, then attempted one of seventy ways to vanquish their opponents in an encounter that might last no longer than a few seconds. Hokutoumi won the event and among the contestants was Konishiki from Hawaii who, at 250kg, was the heaviest contender ever to set foot in a *dhoyo*, and undoubtedly the largest performer to have entered the Hall.

The Hall continued to host large fund-raising events. Fashion Aid followed Live Aid in 1985. Peter Stringfellow, the nightclub owner, paid the £5,000 hire of the Hall and among the 125 models was Jerry Hall, who stepped out of a foil-wrapped box in a red and gold lamé strapless dress. The UK Fashion Awards have subsequently been held in the Hall, as has the L'Oréal Colour Trophy for Britain's best hairdressers. But when it comes to hairstyles and dress, the national ballroom championships, scattering sequins like stardust, out-glitter them all.

The Hall is a place for a big celebration, for birthdays, tributes and other special occasions. The music producer George Martin and friends gave a big pop concert for Montserrat after a volcano devastated the island where he ran Air Studios. Eric Clapton and Paul McCartney turned out again to pay tribute to George Harrison in a concert that sold out in ninety minutes; touts were asking £700 a ticket. McCartney gave a concert in memory of his his wife, Linda. When Andrew Lloyd Webber hired the Hall to celebrate his fiftieth birthday, former leading ladies from his shows sang his songs. Menuhin celebrated the 70th anniversary of his first appearance. Humphrey Burton, former arts supremo of the BBC and author of biographies of Leonard Bernstein and Yehudi Menuhin, hired the Hall to conduct Verdi's Requiem, with five choral societies and the Philharmonia Orchestra, raising £70,000 for the Prostate Research Campaign, UK.

All these occasions provided fodder for columnists and gossip magazines, but the Hall continued to generate real news. The annual meeting of the Institute of Directors usually merits nothing more interesting than photographs of its fellows in their seats eating out of lunch boxes. But in 1991 fellows watched in open-mouthed awe as Gerald Ratner, the high-street jewellery shop magnate, jettisoned his entire empire in just a few words. Talking of his products, he said with suicidal honesty, "We also do cut-glass sherry decanters complete with six glasses on a silver-plated tray that your butler can serve you drinks on – all for £4.95. People say, 'How can you sell this for such a low price?' I say, 'Because it is total crap.' We also sell earrings for under £1, which is cheaper than a prawn sandwich from M&S. But I have to say that the earrings probably won't last as long." The speech wiped £500 million off the value of his company and consigned him to the business wilderness for a considerable period.

More recently, the former US National Security Adviser, Henry Kissinger, was speaking to the Institute of Directors, while outside the Hall, Kensington Gore was blocked by a couple of hundred demonstrators protesting about both globalisation and his involvement in US foreign policy in southeast Asia and Latin

America. Less than two miles away the campaigner Peter Tatchell was applying to Bow Street magistrates for a warrant to have him arrested for alleged war crimes.

Redevelopment and Refurbishment

All these events and occasions had their special requirements, and as the ambitions of performers and promoters increased, the shortcomings of the Victorian Hall became more and more obvious. Conditions for artists were cramped. The North Porch had been glassed in during the 1971 clean-up but no proper entrance on the south side had replaced the Royal Horticultural Society's conservatory that was dismantled towards the end of the 19th century. The whole roof needed reglazing, the organ was worn out, the facilities second rate, storage was at a premium and the seating needed a thorough overhaul. More pressingly, something had to be done about the the "get-ins" and "get-outs", the physical movement of lorry-loads of equipment on to and off the stage. Everything from concert grand pianos to entire sets was loaded through Door 11, from where it had to be manhandled down a three-in-one ramp to the arena.

Then, in 1987, a sign fell from the heavens. A piece of terracotta moulding, weakened by the wet sandblasting of the centenary clean-up and loosened by frost, slipped off the façade from gallery level and crashed on to the the South Porch. It was time serious attention was paid to the building. Press reports that the falling masonry could only mean that the Hall was about to collapse were unfounded, but the same could not be said of the Albert Memorial opposite, which by now was in real danger of disintegration. Albert's fate was debated: one option was demolition. As the then general manager, Cameron McNicol, cheerfully pointed out, unlike the Memorial, the Hall had been designed by engineers, not architects, so there was absolutely no chance of it ever falling down. Nevertheless something – many things – had to be done. Scaffolding went up around the Hall.

While the best way forward for the Hall was being discussed, a second event hastened plans along. The fatal fire at Bradford football stadium brought about tough new regulations to be applied to all public buildings, necessitating urgent work to improve fire safety. By 1991 a more far-reaching and ambitious architectural masterplan to address the Hall's shortcomings had been drawn up under a new Chief Executive, Patrick Deuchar, who had arrived in post in 1989 with a burning conviction of the Hall's potential and the need to revitalise it from top to bottom. He was joined in 1991 by David Elliott as Director of Finance and Administration, a shrewd choice by the Hall, since Elliott's career had combined hard-nosed banking with Barings in London and New York with a spell as Finance Director of the English National Opera. In 1994 Elliott became Deputy Chief Executive of the Hall, and in 1998 succeeded Deuchar as Chief Executive to oversee the implementation of the redevelopment and reconstruction work.

The opportunity to put the masterplan into effect in one high-spending spree did not arise until 1995 when the National Lottery was introduced. This welcome fount of funds was to take most of London's great institutions by the scruff of the neck and shake them down for the 21st century. It also helped to rejuvenate the larger institutions of Albertopolis and it miraculously saved the Albert Memorial, which underwent a full-blown renaissance. The Hall received £40.2 million, leaving £30 million to find. There were generous contributions from patrons, seat holders and charitable trusts. Money-raising evenings were among events that went on throughout the eight years' work. Unlike Sadlers Wells, the Royal Opera House and the Coliseum, which closed during their redevelopment, the Hall's shows had to go on.

The most ambitious part of the plan, worked out by Martin Ward of the architects Building Design Partnership along with the Hall's then Director of Development, Ian Blackburn, was the four-storey excavation beneath the building, extending south to Prince Consort Road with a lorry entrance beside the South Steps. This major piece of civil engineering, managed on behalf of the Hall by Taylor Woodrow Construction, provides vehicle access to a car park and service yard deep beneath the original foundations. This allows equipment to be unloaded and sent up to the auditorium by lift. Excavation of the entire area between the Hall and Prince Consort Road meant the felling of much-loved cherry trees. Their pink blossom had for years brightened each spring, and their demise was the subject of many consultations with the local residents, whose lives are inextricably linked to the Hall. The excavations also meant breaking through the original concrete base of the RHS conservatory and removing the statue of Prince Albert by Joseph Durham, commissioned for the 1851 Great Exhibition, set up in the gardens of the RHS and finally moved to the top of the South Steps after the conservatory was taken down. Two wells and a brick culvert that had supplied water for the RHS ponds and fountains were uncovered. One of the wells had been dug out and bricked to a depth of 140 feet.

All this work had to be carried out without any interruption to the lettings. Only on the two brief occasions when the actual seating in the Hall was stripped out and entirely replaced did the doors close. Throughout 1998 workmen with picks and shovels laboured immediately beneath the stage and arena floor to dig out London shale and clay. During the day contractors often had to cease work during rehearsals although, to make up time in the Proms season, the work continued through rehearsals in secret in what was described by Elliott as like a scene from *The Great Escape*. On one occasion Cliff Richard, a regular at the

Hall, had to be guided through the building works in a hard hat in order to reach the stage.

Lobbies and other new areas of the building were opened up, and bars and restaurants refurbished. A new decorative scheme for the public areas and auditorium was developed by Donald Insall Associates, the pre-eminent firm of conservation architects who had been involved with the restoration of Windsor Castle after the 1992 fire. Colours and patterns for the halls and corridors were matched as far as possible to the originals. Hundreds of yards of curved carpet were ordered and laid.

Sound engineers carried out a three-year study of the Hall's acoustics using a one-twelfth scale model. Notorious when first built, the acoustics had been largely tamed by the suspended mushroom-shaped reflectors in the late 1960s. Repositioning them improved the immediacy of the sound in the auditorium and had the added benefit of revealing the reinstated decorative cove that runs round the base of the dome.

Classical Revival

As the redevelopment of the Hall got under way, it was increasingly clear that it must be able to attract top orchestras throughout the year. Classical music was becoming popular again, as the opening of Birmingham's state-of-the-art Symphony Hall, Manchester's award-winning Bridgewater Hall and the Waterfront Hall in Belfast confirmed.

Classical music had been given a boost during the 1990 football World Cup when the Three Tenors had sent Nessun Dorma, the tenor aria from Puccini's *Turandot*, racing up the popular music charts. CDs were just beginning to replace vinyl and the Three Tenors sparked a twenty percent increase in the sale of classical records. The vogue had, however, been anticipated by Raymond Gubbay, an impressario in the showman mould of C.B. Cochran, who had begun his career working briefly for Victor and Lilian Hochhauser. With such stunts as free entries for children carrying teddy bears, or free flowers for women attending a Valentine concert, Gubbay had become Britain's biggest classical music promoter. In 1989 he put on the first Classic Spectacular at the Hall, based on what he thought were the fifteen most popular pieces of classical music. "It's not a traditional concert," he said at the time. "There's no concerto, no focus point. Just lots and lots of popular tunes that people will know." The event sold out in ten days. It was a winning formula, one that could be seen reflected in the first national independent radio station, Classic FM, which went on air in 1992 with a format that has been copied all around the world.

Other venues opened up. Gubbay staged *Turandot* with the Royal Opera at Wembley Arena. In the summer of 1991 Harvey Goldsmith, a regular rock and pop promoter at the Hall who had moved into staging arena operas, presented a concert by Pavarotti in rain-soaked Hyde Park. Four years later there were Proms in the Park with a screening of the Last Night from the Hall.

The collapse of communism brought a wealth of classical talent from eastern Europe and the former Soviet Union. The Bolshoi Ballet danced for a season. The Romanian National Opera arrived and the Friends of Kirov Opera brought *Prince Igor*, a stunning performance with 200 singers.

Opera in the Round

Anxious to generate more shows and more income, the Hall linked up with Gubbay to put on *La Bohème*. This was the first time that a full opera had been staged in the Hall in the round. Critics were initially sniffy that such a blockbuster could work, but by the time the next joint productions, of *Carmen* and *Madam Butterfly*, came along, they were convinced. With Li Ping Zhang as Butterfly, the Puccini opera was set around a Japanese water garden and when the lights went down and the floating candles glowed for the love duet with Pinkerton, the effect was overwhelming. The London *Evening Standard* ran a headline: "How the beautiful Butterfly moved the Albert Hall to tears".

For this first production of *Butterfly* massive tanks into which the ponds had to drain barely managed to squeeze into the space beneath the arena. For a repeat, sell-out production in 2002, with the new access levels excavated beneath the building, the same task was performed with ease.

The Hall also teamed up with Gubbay to introduce ballet to the arena, starting with *Swan Lake*. Directed by Derek Deane, the £1.8 million production had little by way of sets, but brilliant choreography and a great deal of action, with fire eaters, jugglers and acrobats joining the 120 dancers, twice the usual number for Tchaikovsky's ballet. The English National Ballet provided the corps of ballerinas, with Altynai Asylmuratova, principal of the Kirov, and Roberto Bolle from La Scala, Milan. A high point of the ballet was the seventy swans who made wonderful patterns across the floor. "This is a major achievement," Nicholas Dromgoole wrote in the *Sunday Telegraph*. "Deane has created a new medium." Roberto Bolle returned in 1998 to dance with Tamara Rojo in *Romeo and Juliet*, another Deane blockbuster, set in Renaissance Verona.

The other spectacular which the Hall set out to secure was the Montreal circus troupe, Cirque du Soleil. Forty-five artistes from nine countries and 750 tons of equipment arrived at the Hall on Boxing Day 1996 for their first presentation, "Saltimbanco", as work on the redevelopment was beginning. Ten years earlier Cirque's English director, Andrew Watson, performed his trapeze act for a private party in the Hall. "I thought then that this is the ultimate circus building from the point of its shape, height and possibilities for rigging," he said. Tickets were not cheap, but the show has proved a regular New Year success, helping to fill the traditionally weak period in the Hall's calendar and contributing to the redevelopment fund.

The Final Stages
When the BBC Proms started their 2003 season, tickets went on sale in a new box office reached through the newly-built South Porch. This had long been the runt of the litter, a snub-nosed entrance that had been wedged against the RHS conservatory. By matching the South Porch to its three sisters, it provided an imposing new entrance, with a foyer, shop space and stairs up to a new crescent-shaped restaurant with wonderful views across the South Steps to the Royal College of Music. All was immaculately in keeping, a duochrome of terracotta and brick, with niches for Elizabeth II matching those of her great-great-grandparents, Victoria and Albert, on the North Porch. The only nod to modernity is the tympanum, where a sparkling mosaic by Shelagh Wakeley adds unexpected colour.

Prommers queued on the restored steps; new balustrades line the gardens replanted by Colvin & Moggridge. Coloured gravel has been laid around four young cherry trees ready to blossom for the official opening in the spring of 2004. The final fanfare to mark the completion of the works is the organ. During a £1.4 million refurbishment it was largely removed, rebuilt and reinstalled. All 9,779 pipes of the 150-ton instrument have been cleaned, all its stops refitted. In the summer of 2004 the full "Voice of Jupiter" will once again reverberate around the Hall.

Newly pedestrianised areas of York paving and granite kerbstones opened up around the building and Albert was replaced at the top of the South Steps on his plinth, now housing a ventilation and firefighting shaft. Heating and ventilation for the Hall has all been renewed. Two men dug a fifty-five-metre long shaft, two metres in diameter, to bring fresh air to the centre of the auditorium, which is appreciated by Prommers, many of whom have been coming for years. "Mad Ken" Johnson, for instance, a warehouseman from Bentalls department store in Kingston-upon-Thames, received a glass bowl from his fellow fans on his retirement after attending 1,482 proms over thirty-eight years. Even the ticket touts have remained loyal, although Oliver, who has been hovering by the queues for twenty years, has never once stepped foot inside the Hall.

Most Prommers are, of course, not interested in the comfort of seats. No other concert hall in the world offers the luxury that they enjoy: the cheapest tickets in the house for the best place to be. Their roars of approval and stamping feet are just what performers like to hear. "The proximity of this huge standing crowd, listening in impeccable silence, has a galvanising effect on the finest musician," Richard Morrison wrote in *The Times* in 2003. "They play out of their skins." He maintains that by attending all seventy-odd concerts in a Proms season, reading the programme notes and gauging your own response to the comments and critics, you can learn more about music history and performance in a single summer than a conservatoire or university could teach you in three years. Such a thought would have been music indeed to Prince Albert's ears.

Albert's Hall Today
The Royal Albert Hall is an inspiring, Grade I listed building, with new bars, restaurants and new spaces that can be put to good use. It seats 5,278, including 22 wheelchairs. In a year it consumes 300 litres of paint, 360 metres of carpet laid, 4,800 lightbulbs, 1,000 bottles of gin, 600 of whisky and 5,500 of champagne. A million tickets are sold and the number of seats repaired is the same as the number of days in a year. It is probably chiefly known for the eight-week summer Proms, broadcast live daily on Radio 3, with more concerts than ever on television and as webcasts.

Much more happens at the Royal Albert Hall than the Proms. There are a host of other musical events: Viennese evenings, Sir Malcolm Sargent charity concerts, the Easter Requiem and Christmas Messiah, and contemporary music, such as the week of concerts in aid of The Teenage Cancer Trust, inspired by Roger Daltrey of the Who and featuring idols of today's generation as well as his own. Music is celebrated in annual awards, such as the Classic BRIT awards and the MOBO awards for popular music. The ideals of Prince Albert and Henry Cole continue to be seen: a lecture by Stephen Hawking or the Dalai Lama, degree ceremonies from London University and the Royal College of Art, rigorous advice from the Keep Fit Association. From here books and films are launched on to the world: Harry Potter, *101 Dalmations*, James Bond. It remains a place for reunions and get-togethers, for the Boy Scouts, the Salvation Army, the Christian Girls' and Boys' Brigades, the Methodist Association of Youth Clubs, the World Evangelism Society of Great Britain and the Royal British Legion's Annual Festival of Remembrance attended by the Queen. Her arrival brings out the handsome Hammercloth, which is draped over the front of the Royal Box. Sewn by the Royal School of Needlework in Princes Gate in 1878, it has been repaired by the Royal School, now at Hampton Court Palace, as part of the refurbishments.

This is the nation's village hall, a place for princes and Prommers to get together. To look at what goes on here every night of the year is to glimpse the entire cross section of current British culture. Whatever happens in the 21st century, there will be no better place to see its passing trends, its aspirations, idols and ideas than at the Royal Albert Hall.

Members of the Women's Institute
take a break from their annual
meeting at the feet of Prince Albert.
His Memorial, like his Hall, was in
urgent need of repair.

Above Regular appearances of the English Folk Dance and Song Society included groups from different parts of the world.

Right 'Africa 84' brought traditional, seldom seen music and dance from another continent to the Hall.

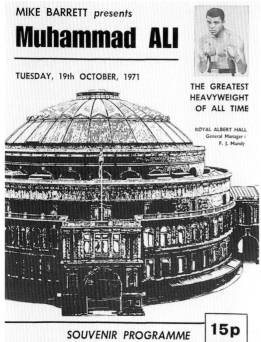

Left Frank Bruno (at the hall in 1991) the incredibly brave and charismatic heavyweight boxer who charmed the nation in the latter part of the last century and won 40 out of 45 professional contests. Known and loved for the catch phrase he used when being interviewed by the BBC Boxing Correspondent, Harry Carpeneter, "Know-wot-I-mean, 'arry?", Bruno has very sadly been afflicted recently by serious health problems.

Muhammad Ali, the great world heavyweight boxing champion, fought an exhibition match in the Hall in 1971. After refusing to be drafted to fight in Vietnam on religious grounds, his boxing licence had been suspended and he had been out of the game for three years. He went on to regain the title in 1974.

Left Petula Clark has made several appearances at the Hall. At her 40th anniversary concert in 1983 she sang with the London Philharmonic Orchestra in aid of the LPO National Appeal Fund.

Right In her shimmering gowns, Dame Shirley Bassey has proved to be one of the most popular female singers to appear at the Hall. This concert was in 1973. She starred in a concert given for Prince Philip's eightieth birthday in 2001, leading the singing of 'Happy Birthday'.

Tickets to Frank Sinatra concerts were among the most expensive that touts have ever laid their hands on. The Americn crooner was always at home in 'Francis Albert Hall' where he first sang in 1975, appearing regularly for the next seventeen years. In 1989 he shared the stage with Liza Minnelli and Sammy Davis Jr (*right*) in a concert that was billed as The Ultimate Event. For many fans, that is exactly what it was.

Above Versatile André Previn rehearses a carol concert at the Hall in 1973 with Julie Andrews and the London Symphony Orchestra, which he directed from 1969 to 1979. He received an honorary KBE in 1996.

Right Leonard Bernstein was guest conductor of the London Symphony Orchestra at the Hall in 1970. His physical leaps and volatile style rather shocked the British audience when he first conducted at the Hall in 1947. In 1988 he organised and conducted a *Songfest* for his 70th birthday.

Above Engaging and enthusiastic, Sir Simon Rattle conducts at a sell-out concert of Mahler's Symphony No. 8 with the National Youth Orchestra in 2002. The following year he brought the Berlin Philharmonic Orchestra to the Proms.

Right Sir Adrian Boult at the Hall in 1976. The antithesis of Bernstein, Boult was an essentially English conductor who made the minimum of fuss. He is regarded as the architect of the BBC Symphony Orchestra; he was its Conductor from 1930 to 1950 and the BBC's Director of Music between 1930 and 1942.

Hungarian-born Sir Georg Solti rehearses the Chicago Symphony Orchestra in 1978; he was the CSO's music director from 1969 to 1992. Sometimes bombastic, often very tense, he was seen as the last of the 20th century's 'superconductors' after Bernstein and Herbert von Karajan.

Sir John (Giovanni Battista)
Barbirolli, the son and grandson
of Italian violists with La Scala
Orchestra in Milan, was permanent
conductor of Manchester's Hallé
Orchestra from 1943 to 1958, one
of the first outside orchestras to be
invited to play at the Proms.

Above José Carreras pays tribute to Hollywood tenor Mario Lanza with the BBC Concert Orchestra, 1994.

Right Luciano Pavarotti at a 1982 Royal Gala rehearsal for the Royal Philharmonic Orchestra Appeal attended by the Queen Mother.

Opposite In 1983, after a decade apart, the Everly Brothers, Don and Phil, chose the Royal Albert Hall for their reunion concert.

LONDON 21-27 February 1976   Price 10p
BBC Radio London: page 58

RadioTimes

Raising the roof

Back feature:
How the British entry for the
Eurovision Song Contest is
being chosen this year
— in A Song
for Europe,
live from
the Albert Hall,
Wednesday
BBC1

Talents to amuse: Australia's Edna Everage (*above left*) Denmark's Victor Borge (*above*) and Lancashire's Victoria Wood (*left*).

Opposite The *Radio Times* cover for A Song for Europe, which was held at the Hall to choose Britain's entry for the 1976 Eurovision Song Contest. *Save Your Kisses For Me* by The Brotherhood Of Man was selected and it went on to win the contest in the Netherlands.

Basketball is one of the many regular
sporting fixtures. Badminton and
squash have been played here, too.
The American tennis star, John
McEnroe, has described the Hall as
'the most beautiful setting for indoor
tennis in the world'.

SUMO

THE GRAND **TOURNAMENT**

The Royal Albert Hall
9·13 October 1991

The Royal Albert Hall was the first place in the world outside Japan to hold a Sumo wrestling tournament. It took place in October 1991 as part of a nationwide Japan Festival, and it included the most enormous performers ever seen in the Hall.

Religion becomes performance art with the whirling skirts of the Mevlevi dervishes. Their dance and music, called *sama*, is a spritual oratorio performed by Sufists from Turkey, dating from the 13th century. The dervishes represent the planets revolving around the sun.

'Saltimbanco', Cirque du Soleil's first
show in the Hall, arrived in 1996.
The Royal Albert Hall is the only
theatre in the world in which Cirque
du Soleil performs its touring shows,
usually held in its trademark Grand
Chapiteau. The circus quickly became
a major London show.

Overleaf The ritual Last Night of
the Proms when Britannia rules,
Union flags wave, streamers fly and
the balloons go up. Mark Elder
(*top left*) conducts the orchestra, and
Sir Andrew Davis (*bottom right*)
conducts the Prommers, who have
been described as 'one of the great
listening publics in the world'.

BILLY AND ALBERT

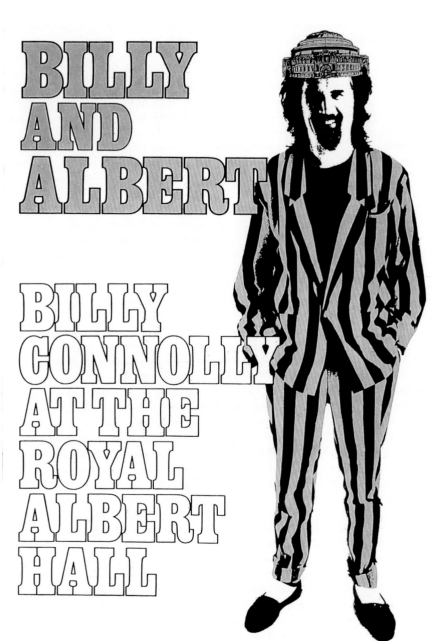

BILLY CONNOLLY AT THE ROYAL ALBERT HALL

Above The comedian Billy Connolly has made several appearances at the Hall. On this occasion Albert Hall hats were issued to the audience to surprise him on the last night of his week-long engagement.

```
Tonight is the last night of Billy's
     week at the Royal Albert Hall.
Billy is unaware that hats are being provided
 for the audience. Although it's obviously not
 compulsory it would be greatly appreciated if
you would welcome him to the stage by placing this
  hat on your head when the house lights go down.
            MANY THANKS!!
```

The Butterfly Ball

a concert in aid of

ACTION RESEARCH
FOR THE CRIPPLED
CHILD

BUD FLANAGAN
LEUKAEMIA
FUND

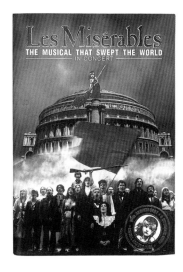

Above Based on a book of poems by
William Plomer illustrated by Alan
Aldridge, *The Butterfly Ball* was
turned into a musical by Roger
Glover and performed for charity.

Above left Every autumn the Schools
Proms perform a variety of work.

Left 1950s rock-and-roller Fats
Domino, still going strong in 1986.

Far left The tenth anniversary of the
West End musical *Les Misérables* was
celebrated at the Hall in 1995.

Top row Sir Cliff Richard, whose many appearances include a 40th anniversary concert; former Beatle Paul McCartney, who hired the Hall for a concert in memory of his wife, Linda; and Cuban Ibrahim Ferrer, still packing the Hall in his seventies.

Middle row Irish flautist James Galway; violinist Vanessa Mae, Best Female Artist in the 1996 BRIT Awards; and Sting, a regular visitor.

Bottom row 'King of the Blues' B.B. King; singer-composer Stevie Wonder; and rock band Genesis.

Top row Eric Clapton, who made
the Hall a venue for annual concerts;
Tina Turner, 'Lifetime Achievement'
winner of the 1999 MOBO awards;
and the versatile Nitin Sawhney.

Middle row George Benson brings
heart and soul; Oasis's Liam
Gallagher, 1990s headline maker;
and Coldplay's Chris Martin.

Bottom row Sir Elton John, stallwart
of Stonewall and other charity
concerts; James Brown, the perennial
'Godfather of soul'; and soulful singer
Craig David.

Left The famous 'Poppy Drop' at the annual British Legion Festival of Remembrance Service.

Right Li Ping Zhang as Cio-Cio-San in the stunning 1998 production of Puccini's opera, *Madam Butterfly*. It moved many of the audience to tears.

Left Directed by Derek Deane in 1997, *Swan Lake* was a major ballet production at the Hall. A few of the dozens of English National Ballet swans are here encircling their patron, Diana, Princess of Wales.

Right Erina Takahashi and Dmitri Gruzdyev with the English National Ballet's *Sleeping Beauty* in 2000. Ballet has proved to be enormously popular at the Hall.

Above Spots on the wall for the 1996 premiere of Disney's *101 Dalmations*.

Left The 2002 royal premiere of the twentieth James Bond film, *Die Another Day,* celebrated the Bond series' fortieth birthday. The Queen and Duke of Edinburgh were joined in the Royal Box by the stars, Pierce Brosnan and Halle Berry.

Right J.K. Rowling reads extracts from *Harry Potter and The Order of Phoenix* and was interviewed by Stephen Fry at the book's launch in June 2003.

Above During the eight-year redevelopment programme the stall seats were entirely replaced. This was one of only two brief occasions when the Hall was closed during the refurbishment.

Left Pulling out all the stops, £1.4 million is being spent on a complete overhaul of the 150-ton organ, to re-establish it as one of the largest, finest and tonally most comprehensive instruments in the world. A new work has been commissioned for its inaugural concert in 2004.

Below Looking down from the Hall towards the Royal College of Music.

Opposite The major civil engineering feat of the £70 million redevelopment was the excavation of four storeys beneath the South Steps for plant rooms and a service yard, so that equipment could be moved easily in and out of the Hall. In spite of the disruption, shows still had to go on.

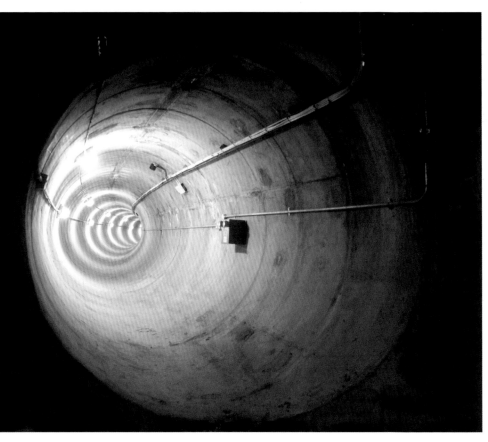

Above As part of the new heating and ventilation system, a 55-metre-long air tunnel, two metres wide, was dug beneath the Hall by just two men to bring fresh air to the centre of the auditorium.

Right The South Steps restored, with replanted gardens and cherry trees. Prince Albert is back on his plinth and the newly-built South Porch now matches the other three porches. In the tympanum, Shelagh Wakeley's mosaic adds a splash of colour. On the first floor the new Café Consort has wonderful views. The vehicle access to the subterranean floors can be seen on the left. Prommers queued on the rebuilt South Steps for the first time during the BBC Proms 2003 season. Forty-five minutes before the performance began, the desk opened for business at Door 11, selling arena and gallery tickets at £4 each, cash only. Those wanting a seat, or who want to book tickets for future events, now make for the new box office through the South Porch, which is open from 9am to 9pm daily. A shop will soon be opened alongside the box office.

DELIVERIES ONLY NO PUBLIC ACCESS

DELIVERIES
No Public Access

Bibliography

Much of the information in this book comes from the Royal Albert Hall's extensive archives, which hold many of the programmes of the actual events, as well as records of Council meetings and newspaper cuttings. An invaluable source of help has been The Gas Book. Kept by a caretaker of the Hall and donated to the archivist, Jacky Cowdrey, on his retirement, the book records the amount of gas consumed by the various hirers of the Hall, providing an infallible way of dating events. The following books also provided helpful information.

Adelina Patti: Queen of Hearts by John Frederick Cone, Scolar Press, 1994.

Edward Elgar: A Creative Life by Jerrold Northrop Moore, Clarendon Press 1999.

Edwina Mountbatten, A Life of Her Own by Janet Morgan, HarperCollins, 1991.

Fourteen Letters by Feliks Topolski, Faber & Faber 1988.

In the Sixties by Barry Miles, Jonathan Cape, 2002.

Land of Sport and Glory by Derek Birlet, Manchester University Press, 1995.

Menuhin: A Life by Humphrey Burton, Faber and Faber, 2001.

Nineteenth Century Britain, Integration and Discovery by Keith Robbin, Clarendon Press, 1988.

Pleasure and Pastimes in Victorian Britain by Pamela Horn, Sutton Publishing, Stroud, 1999.

Prince Albert and the Victorian Age edited by John A.S. Philips from a seminar in Coburg, 1980, Cambridge University Press.

Queen's Hall 1893–1941 by Robert Elkin with a forward by Dr Malcolm Sargent, Rider & Co. Profits from the book were "devoted to the Henry Wood Jubilee Fund for the building a new Concert hall in London".

The Albert Memorial edited by Charles Brooks, published in association with English Heritage and the Paul Mellor Centre for Studies in British Art by Yale University Press, 2000.

The Annals of Covent Garden Theatre by Henry Saxe Wyndham, Chatto and Windus, 1896.

The Hiawatha Man: The Life and Work of Samuel Coleridge-Taylor, 1875–1912 by Geoffrey Self, Scolar Press, 1995.

The History of Broadcasting in the United Kingdom by Asa Briggs, Oxford Universtity Press, 1995.

The Proms by Leslie Ayre, forward by Sir Adrian Boult, Leslie Frewin, 1968.

The Royal Albert Hall by John Richard Thackrah, Terence Dalton Ltd, Suffolk, 1983.

The Royal Albert Hall by Ronald W. Clark, Hamish Hamilton, London 1958. This gives a detailed account of the founding and running of the Hall.

The Royal Albert Hall Campaign 1944 Addresses given during a sixteen-days' campaign by Faith for the Times, Pickering and Inglis, 1944.

The Stones by Philip Norman, Hamish Hamilton, 1984.

Tunes of Glory: The Life of Malcolm Sargent by Richard Aldous, Hutchinson, London 2001.

Discography

There have been hundreds of recordings of concerts at the Hall, and many can be found through specialist music outlets. The following CDs are currently available and give a flavour of the music that has been sung and played at the Hall during the past century.

24 Nights: Eric Clapton (Warner)
Two CDs recorded during the guitarist's 1990–91 series at the Hall. He made regular appearances throughout the 1990s.

Andrew Lloyd Weber: The Royal Albert Hall Celebration
At the composer's 50th birthday party all his stars pass before his eyes, from Elaine Page to Kiri Te Kanawa. Also on DVD.

BBC Proms Centenary 1895–1995 (BBC)
A two-disc compilation from the centenary year. The BBC has a number of Proms CDs, as well as a DVD of the Last Night from 2000, conducted by Sir Andrew Davis.

BBC Proms in the Park (BBC)
Crowd pleasers conducted by Robin Stapleton including Tchaikovsky's *Nutcracker* and Coates' *Dam Busters March*, *Rhapsody in Blue*, and Waltz from *Sleeping Beauty*.

Beethoven: Violin Concerto; Mozart's Sinfonia Concertante (BBC Legends)
This CD has preserved a concert given in September 1963 at the Royal Albert Hall with violin maestros Yehudi Menuhin and David and Igor Oistrakh. There are a number of memorable recordings from the Hall in the BBC Legends series.

The Best Proms Album in the World...Ever! (Virgin)
Sir Charles Mackerras, Sir Neville Mariner conduct on two CDs that includes works from Taverner to Last Night favourites.

Clara Butt: A Critical Survey. Vol. 1: The Acoustic Years and *The Complete Adelina Patti and Victor Maurel (Marston)* 412 North Chester Road, Swarthmore, PA 19081, USA. www.marstonrecords.com Two-set CDs with the recordings of these early opera stars.

Elgar: Violin Concerto and 'Enigma' Concerto (EMI Classics)
This is the recording of 16-year-old Yehudi Menuhin conducted by Edward Elgar with the Royal Albert Hall Orchestra made at No 1 Studio Abbey Road on 15 July 1932, immediately after their performance in the Hall.

Epic Brass (SP&S)
Highlights of the 2001 Nationals Finals Gala Concert from the Royal Albert Hall with the the winning Black Dyke Mills Band, the Salvation Army and Symphonic Brass of London.

Kiri! (United Artists)
A 1994 concert by the New Zealand soprano for her fiftieth birthday, with the London Symphony Orchestra.

Les Misérables 10th Anniversary Concert (Relativity)
The 1995 concert that celebrated the West End musical's first decade, with a cast of 250. Also on video.

Liszt Organ Music: Jennifer Bate
www.classical-artists.com/jbate
The Hall's organ played at the start of the 1974 prom by one of the instrument's finest performers.

Live at the Albert Hall: Bob Dylan (Columbia)
Seminal Dylan CD from the 1966 tour when folk met rock and upset many fans.

Live at the Albert Hall: Ladysmith Black Mambazo (Sanachie)
The first live recording of the famous South African group at a sell-out concert.

Live at the Royal Albert Hall: The Who (Spv)
A box set of three CDs of the band's annual charity concerts for the Teenage Cancer Trust. Roger Daltrey and Pete Townshend are joined by Paul Weller and Nigel Kennedy.

Live at the Royal Albert Hall: Vanessa Mae (EMI)
On her 'Red Hot Tour', the versatile violinist plays folk, rock and classic on acoustic and electric guitar. Also on video.

Myra Hess in Concert 1949–1960 (Music & Program, US)
A four-CD set of the pianist, with the BBC Symphony Orchestra conducted by Sir Adrian Boult, among others.

My Heart and I – Richard Tauber (Gala)
The great Mozart tenor was a popular performer in the 1930s and 40s, making more than 700 recordings.

Olde English Christmas (Laserlight)
One of several Christmas Carol CDs by the Royal Choral Society, conducted by Sir Malcolm Sargent.

Reunion At the Albert Hall: The Everly Brothers (Pie)
Back together after 10 years, this milestone event is also available on DVD.

Robbie Williams Live at the Albert Hall (EMI)
A batch of rat-pack songs and swing songs from the 1950s recorded in 2001, including a duet with a Sinatra recording. Also on DVD

The Song of Hiawatha (Decca)
This recent two-CD recording of the complete song cycle is by the Welsh National Opera and Chorus with Helen Field, Arthur Davies and Bryn Terfel.

Wagner: Tristan und Isolde – Kirsten Flagstad (EMI Classics)
A three-CD set by 'The Voice of the Century', conducted by Furtwängler. For other CDs contact the Kirsten Flagstad Museum:
www.max.no/kultur/flagstad

Acknowledgements

This book was made possible through the co-operation of the management and staff of the Royal Albert Hall under its chief executive, David Elliott, who gave every possible assistance. Most of the material comes from the Royal Albert Hall's extensive archives, maintained by the Hall's archivist, Jacky Cowdrey, who has been unstinting in her help throughout the project. Thanks, too, to her assistant, Alex Collinson, and to Michele Finley, Sarah Woods and Peter Howell in the offices of the Hall. Thalia Stone has helped in numerous ways with the book and thanks are also due to her.

Picture Credits
Except for those listed below, all pictures were supplied from the archives of the Royal Albert Hall and their principal photographer, Chris Christodoulou, who also photographed the posters and programmes for the book. All the colour photographs of performers and events at the Hall are his. The following pictures, and permissions, came from other sources.

Page 4: Clive Barda.
Page 16: Paintings on loan from the Royal Naval Trophy Centre.
Pages 52, 70 (bottom), 71, 72, 91 (right), 92, 95, 107 (top-right) 113, 123, 125 (right), 132, 133: Hulton Getty.
Page 69 (bottom): Popperfoto.
Pages 69 (top), 70 (top), 93: Topham.
Page 83 (bottom right): Joseph Lee/Associated Newspapers.
Page 99, 100-101: The Estate of Feliks Topolski.
Page 104: Illustration by Alan Aldridge and Harry Willock.

Page 130 (bottom), 131 (bottom): Clive Barda/Arena-PAL.
Page 136: Lyn Gray for *Radio Times*.
Pages 142-3: Chris Christodoulou/BBC Proms.
Page 145 (right): *Butterfly Ball* by Alan Aldridge; *Les Misérables* (bottom left) courtesy of CMOL/ Dewynters.
Page 146 (bottom centre): Stevie Wonder/Rose Smith.
Page 147 (bottom right), 149: Phil Dent.
Page 148: Courtesy of the Royal British Legion.
Page 150: Peter Nicholls /NI Syndication.
Page 154, 155 (top), 156: Courtesy of BDP by David Barbour.
Page 157: Photomontage by Terry Barker courtesy of BDP.

All reasonable efforts have been made to trace copyright holders of photographs. We apologise to any that we have not been able to trace.

Edited by Jonathan Stone
Jonathan Stone has written and edited numerous books and articles on drawings, silver (his specialist subject), sculpture and the law (his former profession). His book publishers have included the Oxford University Press, Phaidon Press, Hutchinson, and Lund Humphries; journals and newspapers have included *The Times*, *Sunday Times*, *Conoisseur*, *Apollo*, *Antiques* (USA) and *Goya* (Spain). He has a keen interest in typography and has worked with many of the best-known graphic designers, including Fletcher/Forbes/Gill. He is very pleased to have worked on this book with two very young and talented designers, David Hawkins and Glenn Howard, and for the cover with Alan Kitching, one of the elder statesmen of the profession.

Text by Roger Williams
Roger Williams is the author and editor of a number of guide books, including *Insight Guide: London* and Dorling Kindersley's *London Top Ten*. He also wrote *Time Traveller*, a history of newspaper and periodical publishing, and his novels include *Lunch with Elizabeth David*. He is an Associate Editor of *Cornucopia*.

Picture research by Suzanne Hodgart
Suzanne Hodgart was Arts Editor (1978-82) and Picture Editor (1985-93) of the Sunday Times Magazine. Since then she has been a photography consultant on a number of books including Sebastião Salgado's *Workers*, *The American Century* by Harold Evans, *The Queen Mother's Century* by Robert Lacey and *Home: the Twentieth-century House* by Deyan Sudjic and many Time-Life publications.